GW01279459

The Whole Human

The Whole Human

Interconnecting Modern Life

Luna Gladman

NDP

NEW DEGREE PRESS

COPYRIGHT © 2022 LUNA GLADMAN

All rights reserved.

THE WHOLE HUMAN

Interconnecting Modern Life

ISBN 979-8-88504-579-7 *Paperback*

979-8-88504-924-5 *Kindle Ebook*

979-8-88504-695-4 *Ebook*

When one link breaks, the entire chain falls apart. In memory of H, whose suicide reminds me daily why wholeness is so important.

Contents

Introduction

When I left my entire life behind in London, I expected a huge, eye-opening, explosive experience that would give me absolute clarity about the new direction I needed to go. I would then get my happily ever after living with my prince in my castle. Simple, right?

What actually happened was that a naive, protected city girl marched out into the wilderness with zero experience of this type of terrain nor any of the tools necessary to support this type of venture. It also turned out that the tricky wilderness was not the physical terrain I covered during my travels but instead the landscape inside myself.

As I journeyed over the next five years after leaving London, it felt like being rattled about in a snow globe, shaking up everything I thought I knew. It was turbulent being shaken up like this. But, just like when a snow globe is put down, the snow began to settle, revealing a new landscape—one that supported my daily living. This landscape is my personal perspective on life. Each time the snow globe shakes, it comes back to settle with a new landscape, a new perspective. I did not know who or what shook the snow globe, much like I did not know who or what was directing the universe. However, over time I came to accept that it shakes regularly as a natural part of inhabiting this globe, so my life has shifted to pay attention to what is needed to ride through these storms.

Even better, I wanted to be able to live while being in the storm, rather than battening down the hatches and waiting for the snow to settle at another point in time, which could be a long time to wait. We've all experienced this feeling at some point, right? As though we're in survival mode, just getting by each day, when instead we could be embracing each moment in our lives.

Before leaving London, I had done what I thought I was supposed to do to ensure good health and happiness, only to wake up one morning realizing I was desperately unhappy, in poor health, and could not continue anymore. When starting this new chapter in my life, I felt broken and in a state of despair. I had worked mostly to live at another point in time. Unable to bear listening to myself, I could not sit still for five minutes. Obeying the rules, following the system pre-set by society or the prevalent culture instead of listening to my own self resulted in the disconnection of many parts of me. I was extremely lonely. Believing only in logic backed by science, I denied the possible existence of anything else. I focused on combating the physical symptoms I was experiencing.

In the end, I was in so much conflict, which resulted in ill health that led to the first major shake of the snow globe.

Yet it was this ill health that became so unbearable that paradoxically became my savior at the same time; I had no other option but to gradually include all the parts of my life I had previously denied or ignored. This meant acknowledging the mental, emotional, as well as spiritual aspects of my health—the Whole Human. It involved different approaches, almost sidestepping the physical symptoms to understand the real constraints to my health that actually improved it.

There is a lot more going on than what appears at the surface level. Most of my insights supporting my health came not from a scientific understanding but from an experiential understanding. It was in learning all this that I finally found the will to live. Instead of rejecting life, it has become a continual process of acknowledging, listening, then rebalancing until I come back to the point of harmony. In loving the parts I found frustrating, irritating, or annoying, I found that my health improved, not deteriorated.

In turn, this completely changed my perspective on life as well as the universe itself to be the unguarded inclusion of absolutely everything, including our uniqueness. In the broadest sense, this, to me, is Wholeness. Throughout my journey, I learned numerous ideas about Wholeness that we will explore. I began to see each of our lives as our own personal journeys, which we live out in our own unique way. We are all experiencing life together as part of one integrated, connected universe.

This has led me to question many aspects of modern western life. Is it really supporting me or others to live a healthy life?

So much of my life had been based on implicit cultural ideas of standardization, separation, obedience, being right, endless doing, or listening to external authorities. This was at the expense of an exciting journey of discovering who I really am by engaging in a journey toward Wholeness.

The fabric of western society is breaking down. In their book *Limits To Growth*, Donella Meadows and Jorgan Randers state that "we lack the perspectives, cultural norms, the habits and the institutions required to cope." They refer to "overshoots" that lead to either crashing or careful correction. From their perspective, these overshoots stem from a belief that economic growth increases welfare. I believe that welfare can be changed by seeing things differently, which then impacts how we choose to live our lives, which has a knock-on impact on the systems we utilize.

This type of large-scale cultural change starts within each of us.

Many modern western companies and jobs do not seem to support the Whole Human. According to research conducted by the employee experience company Limeade, during "The Great Resignation" in the US between March and July 2021, 28 percent of people left their job when they did not even have another job lined up. Reasons cited for leaving jobs were burnout, lack of flexibility, not being valued, or an employee feeling as if their well-being was not being supported by the company.

Certain illnesses have skyrocketed in recent years. For example, worldwide obesity has nearly tripled since 1975, with 2.8

million deaths each year, and the number of people with diabetes rose from 108 to 422 million between 1980 and 2014, respectively, according to the World Health Organization. Science Daily indicates that the number of people with heart failure doubled between 1990 and 2017, from 33.5 million to 64.3 million, respectively. For all the growth advocated so strongly by many governments around the world, or for the innovation that many seem to believe is so important to live our lives, we do not appear to be getting any healthier.

Doctor Rangan Chatterjee, a medical doctor with around twenty years of experience, has written five books and leads the UK TV series *Doctor in the House*. He focuses on understanding the real causes behind chronic illnesses that are on the rise in western society. He was in conversation with Jonny Wilkinson, a former England rugby player who, having faced his own mental health challenges, launched the podcast *I Am* to redefine what health, well-being, relationships, and the concept of "human potential" mean. Doctor Chatterjee remarked that the type of care available in western medicine may have been appropriate fifty years ago, when most visits were for acute illnesses; however, nowadays, many of his patients turn up with chronic illnesses caused by lifestyle problems.

Doctor Chatterjee points out that these types of challenges cannot usually be solved by prescribing pills; these require deeper intervention through understanding the connections between everything that is happening with the patient in the context of their environment. In other words, seeing the patient as a Whole Human, connected to the environment they are living in. I saw and experienced the difference this type of approach makes firsthand.

All these instances where the fabric of society is breaking down were also where I was breaking down. As the fabric of myself appeared to fray, journeying toward Wholeness has helped me to weave seamlessly back in. Could a journey toward our own Wholeness be the key to harmony in society?

In the first part of this book, I will share the disillusioned state I was in that led to breaking down. After leaving to travel, along my journey, I discovered the beautiful ancient holistic medicine, Ayurveda. This discovery is what really broke me open to explore that nature of Wholeness and why it is so important in daily life.

In part two, I will share what I learnt about this beautiful ancient medicine that brought an entirely different, intuitive methodology with which to understand the Wholeness of life. This period was like pressing a reset button. I started to see my life as unique. It was also a time where I began really listening to what was going on inside me. It enabled me to notice where I was disconnected. This initiated a desire to dig deeper into myself because I was still struggling to recover my own sense of good health; yet, as I began to experience the benefits of this connected exploration, I wanted to do more of it. This opened opportunities to connect beyond anything I could have imagined.

It was at this point, in part three, that I will share what I began to notice not only with the connections within me impacting my health but also the connections around me.

We are connected in many different ways. The biggest eye-opener for me was seeing how the views of society influenced my own approach to health, as well as the complicated networks of connections we are all a part of. Also, I experienced firsthand how connections to both the masculine and feminine energy are critical for balance in life.

Over time, deeper listening unveiled the true causes behind feeling so constricted as well as where I was limiting myself in daily life. I began to notice different ways I had unwittingly been too caught up in the experience, leaving no space to see what was really going on beneath the surface. As a result of this lack of "space," I did not connect properly to different parts of me, which resulted in feeling broken.

In part four of this book, I will share some of the critical moments in my journey that helped me to see what was really going on underneath. This opened up opportunities to bring myself back into balance. I discovered so many aspects of the universe completely disregarded throughout my childhood. These further changed the nature of my connections with myself, which have resulted in an ever-increasing sense of freedom in life.

The final part of this book, part five, will serve as the conclusion of my journey so far. It contains a few examples of pioneers approaching life, especially in business, from a Whole Human perspective. I wanted to share what they are doing because they illustrate how approaching life from this perspective has the potential to impact the whole of humanity.

This multidimensional exploration has greatly improved my health and finally ignited a desire to actually live life. However, I share parts of my journey not because I believe it is the right perspective to live a healthy life but rather because I find this perspective about life supports me personally. It is my hope it encourages a more inquisitive exploration of whatever is arising in your own life right now.

My life cannot be replicated, so it is not a book containing information for you to copy. Rather, it is a book with stories and insights I learned, along with reflections at the end of each chapter, so you can explore the curiosity that sparks within you.

To me, questioning is a critical first step; I found so many answers by asking the right questions. I have been exposed to many young entrepreneurs with innovative environmental- or humanitarian-focused solutions over the last few years. They often design solutions yet then go back to find what the problem is they are actually solving. It is my belief that asking the right questions enables the identification of actual problems that opens up exploration to identify the root causes. It is understanding these that paves the way to live as a united and healthy humanity.

Wholeness is not a predefined, theoretical, abstract, or even definite concept. It is an undefinable, practical, personal, yet constantly evolving journey. I wanted to share my fascination as well as frustrations with my own exploration of Wholeness.

This book is primarily for those questioning the approach of western city life or who feel that the current western systems are not working yet are unsure that anything can ever actually change. It is for those who have had enough of constantly striving to do more to be enough in the modern world. Or, perhaps you already believe that we are one connected mind, body, and soul, and yet feel disconnected from it or do not understand how this can positively impact your life on a practical level.

You might already be engaged in a lot of self-development yet, at the same time, are exhausted by all these activities but cannot identify why. It is for those who believe more harmony within ourselves and between each other is possible even if we do not know how. You might be afraid to openly discuss your intuition, your soul, or perhaps your spirituality. It is for those who believe in the natural flow of life yet feel constricted by the enormous global processes and systems that attempt to dominate our lives.

The time is coming to connect with all of it. The time is coming in humanity's evolution to reconnect and *re*-member who we really are.

Over time I realized the journey toward Wholeness was not a journey toward a fairy tale life but a journey to embrace all parts of life equally as they arise. This allows a way through the suffering and back to harmony. It is a journey to understand for ourselves who we are, not who we have been told to be. For me, it is a journey that is well and truly underway and will be for the rest of my days.

Would you like to join me?

PART 1

BREAKING: FROM DESTRUCTION TO HOPE

CHAPTER 1

Starting the Journey

Before I began my own personal journey toward Wholeness, I had little desire to live.

In my early years, I went to bed most nights praying I would not wake up. Suicidal ideation was a regular part of my thought patterns. I did not "fit in" at school; I was not welcome with the cool kids but did not gel with others either, although they were kind to me. As a teenager and on into my early twenties, I self-harmed, sometimes cutting or bruising myself out of sheer frustration. The turbulent time I was having was reflected in my physical health. I was often ill growing up, including hospitalization with glandular fever when I was sixteen years old; it took me years to recover properly.

By the time I recovered from this, different physical symptoms had developed in the form of Irritable Bowel Syndrome (IBS), general fatigue, debilitating migraines, as well as other frequent infections. I would then go to the doctor for another round of antibiotics or whatever would make the current infection go away as quickly as possible.

I felt broken—as if there must be something wrong with me. I suffered in silence, not communicating with a single person how I truly felt, which created a disconnection from others. Whenever I was alone, I felt nothing but despair. So, I kept myself so busy that I did not leave even five minutes to sit with these feelings; it felt like too much pain to bear.

I felt guilty because, on the surface level, everything should have been fine. I received an education at an academically good school, went to university, became a chartered accountant, then got a well-paying job in the banking sector in London. Yet I felt as if I was almost dead inside. I numbed myself to get through the weeks by drinking alcohol or taking drugs. For a time, I felt as if they were the only real joys in my life. I was conflicted because my mind was telling me I *should* be grateful for my life, yet I did not feel grateful for this ever-present, underlying despair.

This apparent conflict was actually indicating there was more happening in my life than I had been told was available to me. I knew there was something deeper; only I did not know what that something was.

I completely burned out a couple of times. I recall one evening, I was working the usual long hours when my major bodily functions began to shut down. At around 9:00 p.m. on a Monday in the summertime, the sun was going down after I had been working fifteen days straight. I was so unwell I could barely look at my computer, so my manager sent me home. That same night I woke bolt upright at 3:00 a.m. to throw up in the bowl I had put beside my bed just in case. I saw the ibuprofen I had taken around sixteen hours earlier, completely undigested. I was shocked because my digestive system had completely shut down. I went to the doctor, who told me this happens when the body is in an extreme "fight or flight" mode.

Instead of taking this seriously, I went back to continuing in my usual unhealthy lifestyle, ignoring deeper underlying issues. I did not want to look at what was really going on. I was anxious a lot of the time, getting sweaty palms before presentations or panicky when speaking with senior management at work. My weight went up and down like a yo-yo, with one colleague remarking that the clothes that fit me a month ago then hung off me the next.

In the end, I was clinging on desperately to life the way I was living it. I didn't want to admit I was struggling or that I could not seem to cope with life when it appeared that everyone else could. I did not think it was okay to say that things were so completely not okay for me. My unwillingness to admit this was precisely the factor that kept me trapped for so many years. Then, one Sunday in January 2016, I finally broke down as I sat on my couch with an all-too-familiar hangover. The snow globe shook violently. Looking outside my window, watching the usual depressing London rain, I admitted to myself:

"I can't go on like this. I don't know what to do."

I was completely broken from my current way of life. When I acknowledged this, it felt like a dark and lonely position to be in. Yet I felt a strange sense of liberation as well as a greater liberation to come. Finally, there was a glimmer of hope. It was the first of many awakening moments over the next six years that took me into a life beyond anything I had ever imagined. When I look back, admitting "I don't know" was one of the most pivotal moments of my life. Even though I admitted I could not go on like this out of desperation, it also meant I was now willing to consider alternatives. If the life I thought I was supposed to lead did not work, then I had to find alternative ways that did work.

I did not want to die, not really. What I wanted was the desire to live. I wanted to feel Whole.

What had happened with this acknowledgment was that my true nature was beginning to assert itself once more after years of suppressing it. I gradually opened up to listening to different ideas on life itself that I would not have listened to otherwise. It was also the first of many pivotal moments where the seemingly dark, desperate moments of confusion or disillusionment opened the way to explore more deeply who I am, gradually feeling lighter, happier, and more Whole. It is my belief that we are all of it; the light *and* the dark.

I had been following a path defined by society or expectations from others about how I should be living. I thought if I could just continue like everyone else, if I could just play the corporate game like everyone else, if I kept myself going with short-lived relief in the form of alcohol or drugs like everyone else, that somehow, yes, it would all turn out fine.

Only, I am not everyone else.

I had constantly been seeking guidance from *external* sources; from family, school, university, my managers, as well as the prevalent attitudes of society. This moment, when I said, "I don't know," marked the point where I began to turn my priorities inward.

Let's begin with what happened after I acknowledged I could not go on living my life the way I had been living it. Although I felt broken, I knew I wanted to feel Whole.

The journey had begun.

***

Reflection

When I look back, admitting to myself that "I can't go on like this. I don't know what to do" was the single most supportive moment of my entire life. It sent me in an entirely new direction, not because I had any answers, but because I fully acknowledged my current situation. This opened the gateway to exploring something completely different that, as we shall see throughout this book, after many twists and turns, resulted in a desire to live life.

- Are there aspects of your life that you know are not working, yet you keep doing because you don't know what else to do?
  - What are they?

You do not need to have any answers yet; you only need to be honest with yourself about where you are right now.

CHAPTER 2

Finding Hope

As I left London to go traveling in March 2016, it marked a shift from a life I thought I was supposed to have to one I actually wanted—to experience a sense of freedom and a sense of happiness and Wholeness. I thought that if I left the current environment, then everything would change and be okay. I was now traveling around Latin America, carefree with no responsibilities; how could I not have the time of my life?!

To my dismay, after six months of traveling, most of my physical health symptoms persisted, along with the all-too-familiar feelings of loneliness and despair. I still felt completely broken. I was extremely tired a lot of the time, trying to give the impression to other travelers that I was simply going slow to savor each moment when, in reality, I was struggling to survive with each moment. Even though I was meeting a lot of people, I felt disconnected from them somehow. It was as if things had gotten worse because, adding to these feelings, I now had no anchor in the form of a career, a home to live in, or friends around me.

Up until when I left, I had thought knowing where I was going in my career would bring security, that having my own place to live would bring stability so I could live happily ever after. I knew this had not worked for me, but I did not know what did. I was going round in circles.

"*What is wrong with me?*" was a constant thought.

I started to question more deeply why these symptoms persisted. It felt as if they were stuck in me somehow. I did not believe the western doctors that told me nothing could be done about IBS or migraines, or that it was something I had to live with for the rest of my life. I did not have these problems in childhood; I developed them as an adult. As far as I was concerned, I could, therefore, "un-develop" them.

The problem was I did not know how. I was convinced that the mental-emotional challenges I faced, like anxiety, were linked to my physical symptoms, even though I did not understand the link exactly yet. At the time, I was lost in continual frustration, wondering, "Why me?" I thought it was not fair to be suffering alone like this. One traveler even told me directly to be more positive, as I was complaining, as usual, struggling to climb down a mountain in the foothills of Vilcabamba, Ecuador. It was as if I was completely shrouded in a cloud of darkness.

Then, during my travels in Ecuador, I ended up at a retreat outside Cuenca. In a bizarre twist of events, I met an Ayurveda practitioner who happened to be offering a talk about it. Little did I know that participating in this talk would initiate a completely different type of exploration in my life, one where I could explore who I really am. Ayurveda is an ancient system of medicine originating from India.

The term "Ayurveda" is loosely translated as "*the real knowledge about oneself to lead a healthy, long life.*" The practitioner described how we each have our own unique constitutions. In Ayurveda, each individual is considered to have their own balance point that is harmonic in daily life with itself and the universe. This natural, unique constitution, or in other words, our own balance point, is known as the Prakruti Dosha.

Ayurveda has been practiced in India long before modern scientific methods were available. They devised an intuitive methodology to understand the complex intricacies of the interactions of life. They are based on the elements of life that are ether (or space), air, fire, water, and earth. These are conceptual understandings of different characteristics combining the mind, body, and soul together as one Whole Human in one whole universe.

Absolutely everything is connected in Ayurveda, yet I felt completely broken. I was intrigued:

If I am already Whole, then what is happening that is causing me to feel broken in some way?

The language used is ancient Sanskrit. Often it is difficult to even translate Sanskrit words since they combine physical with nonphysical attributes in the same word. In the English language, we have largely separated out physical and nonphysical attributes, which is also reflected in the separated way western medicine is practiced as well as the way we live our lives.

It was eye-opening for me to realize that there was a way of approaching life that assumes the intertwining of all physical with nonphysical attributes to the point where they are described together in one word. For example, the word "*Ama*" in Sanskrit is often translated to English as toxins in our bodies. However, in English, from a scientific point of view, such toxins usually refer to physical substances that are poisonous. In Ayurveda, *Ama* is understood to combine physical *and* nonphysical characteristics. In other words, nonphysical things can be poisonous too. Our emotions or thoughts, as well as other factors like culture, family patterns, societal norms, and geographical locations could also be harmful, resulting in combined physical and nonphysical toxins residing our body, mind, or soul. It is the build-up of this Ama that eventually causes diseases. Conversely when everything is connected together harmoniously in Ayurveda, there is no Ama of any kind; this is considered good health.

This really grabbed my attention. For the first time, there was a methodology that could explain the root causes behind the pains I was experiencing. Also, for the first time, there was a methodology that potentially could interconnect all the seemingly separate physical, mental and emotional symptoms together in a flow of life. It is possible to assess which element is out of balance to guide ourselves back to balance. Every human is Whole, with all its parts functioning or not functioning together.

For example, in Ayurveda, anxiety is linked to a clear pathology with physical symptoms such as poor digestion, bloating, or constipation, all of which I experienced regularly. The type of migraines I suffered from included loss of vision which are linked with underlying anger, which I often felt but at that time still ignored or suppressed. Good digestion is critical for good health in Ayurveda, so much attention is paid to restoring and maintaining gut health. When digestion is poor, overall health is poor, which explains why I kept getting multiple infections on a regular basis.

As the practitioner explained Ayurveda, it was as if a light bulb switched on; I was beginning to see the light in the darkness that had permeated my life so far. Ayurveda offered possible explanations behind my sense of brokenness as well as connections that opened a possible path to journey toward a sense of Wholeness. Instinctively, I knew I had to find out more.

I wanted to study Ayurveda in sufficient depth so I could guide myself through illnesses or, better yet, stop them from occurring in the first place. Ayurveda places a lot of emphasis on preventing disease instead of curing it, which I was by this time very keen to do. I did not want to be dependent on doctors nor to feel so helpless with my situation. I had had enough of dragging my heels through life. It was also important to me to learn from a source that practiced Ayurveda in a traditional way, keeping true to the ancient texts.

Finally, after a lot of digging, I found Mountain Top Clinic (MTC). From the first communication I received from the Chief Physician at MTC, Dr. Sundara, I had a good feeling about it. It did not take me long to sign up for a residential course. A few months later, after a short stop in Spain, I made my way to this homely clinic nestled in the mountains of Tamil Nadu, ushering in a new chapter in my life.

As the taxi pulled into the tranquil grounds at MTC, my initial plan was to study there for three months. This turned into nearly six months as well as participating in their intensive treatment program. I still feel like I only scratched the surface of Ayurveda knowledge; Ayurveda doctors in India studied for as long as western doctors in order to practice this ancient medicine. In parts of India, Ayurveda hospitals are as big as western hospitals. Still, what I learned at MTC took me years to fully comprehend and digest afterward. It sparked a journey I am still on today.

This place was like pressing a reset button on my life; it would be the years beyond MTC where I began to really rebuild my life. It gave me the hope I needed. What I learned at MTC were the basic but critical foundations that set me on a path to rebalance myself by exploring ever deeper into who I really am. It was the first time I really took a step back to evaluate life in a holistic way. As I settled into my simple yet cozy accommodation, I felt a huge sense of relief to finally be here.

I naively thought this course would quickly solve all my health issues, just like that. Sometimes naivety is an advantageous thing because although what I learned at MTC laid the foundations, it took another few years and many, many lessons later to really recover.

I had absolutely no idea what I had just started nor the frustrating journey I had just begun.

***

Reflection

One of the biggest impacts Ayurveda had on my life was understanding that everything is connected in some way. Nothing happens in isolation from the rest of the system, no matter what type of system.

- Do you have ill health symptoms that could be connected even if you cannot see how?
- Are there parts of your life that are not working as smoothly as you would like, perhaps work or relationships?
  - What are they?
- Consider for a moment that everything is connected. What impact does this perspective have on the things you have noted above?
- Consider what the impact is on you, your family, friends, and humanity if everything is connected.

You do not need to understand how anything might be connected yet. For me, it was a huge relief yet overwhelming at the same time to consider that everything is connected somehow. At this point, it still did not solve anything; it only opened another gateway to explore something beyond surface-level appearances. Over the coming chapters, we will look at what this means and the options that became available when exploring deeper.

PART 2

CONNECTING: FROM CONSTRICTION TO OPPORTUNITIES

CHAPTER 3

Disconnections Seen by Listening

Studies began promptly after my arrival, and I was eager to get immersed in learning the beautiful craft of Ayurveda. Although I studied intensively, the most important takeaways I have from this time are not Ayurveda-specific. They set in motion the beginning of a momentous shift toward a more supportive approach to living my life. It was a shift toward a different exploration of life, to explore the Whole of who I am.

From the beginning, Dr. Sundara encouraged me to listen to my own body, mind, and emotional states on a daily basis. It started at a basic level, a daily diary of food, my pulse, bowel movements, other physical symptoms, emotions, and state of mind. It was a tangible mechanism to focus on where I was at that moment. I also began to look at these symptoms together instead of as independent occurrences. Although later I would start to listen a lot more deeply, this was like an initiation into why listening to ourselves is so important in daily life.

For the first time, I was taking notice of my physical body functions, emotional states, or mental clarity. I also noted what I was ingesting in the form of food or other activities. On days when my digestion was better, I had more energy with slightly better clarity of mind, along with feeling less anxious. On days when my stomach was bloated or I was constipated, I would get a headache (which would sometimes result in a migraine) and feel tired and sluggish, often combined with a general feeling of despair about my situation. I began to notice that the worse my digestion was, the more I felt sorry for myself. Unhelpful inner comments started to reduce when my digestion was better.

When waking up, I noticed that my pulse was often erratic, fast, and weak, accompanied by an underlying feeling of anxiousness as if I was in "fight or flight" mode. I suddenly became very aware that this state of anxiety had felt normal my whole life; I had never questioned or observed this until now.

This daily noticing was so simple to do yet were huge observations because I suddenly became very aware of my own human, fluctuating state. I also became aware of ever-present states that must have been affecting my physical health; anxiousness, for example, is linked to bloating and constipation as part of the characteristics of the element of Air in Ayurveda. As the movement of this element is erratic, so too was my physical state. In turn, I became aware that these states were not natural. They were not who I am; they were instead an imbalance.

According to Ayurveda, at any given time, most of us are experiencing imbalance, known as the "Vikruti dosha," that can result in disease or discomfort of some sort. In Ayurveda pathologies, by the time you are noticing symptoms, *Ama* (as mentioned in the previous chapter) has been building up for some time. Ayurveda lifestyle advice, treatments, and remedies are tailored to rebalancing from the identified imbalances back to your own natural constitution. As the imbalances change and you recover from illness or through progression through life, the Ayurveda advice may therefore change accordingly.

There is standard basic lifestyle advice, but often the advice is tailored to coming back to your natural constitution, which will be your own elemental balance. Instead of standardizing the approach to life, it is personalized to you as a unique human. Each of us is considered unique; therefore, living it involves personalization, not standardization. So life is also about deepening the knowledge about what makes each of us unique, since the more this is understood, the more you can tailor your daily life to support this. I was beginning to understand what Ayurveda meant by the idea of "real knowledge"; it is the knowledge about who I really am instead of what society or anyone else tells me I am supposed to be.

For most of my life, I had focused on acquiring knowledge about who I am from external sources. This was mostly scientific-based information about how a standard body functions along with what it needs. I had focused mainly on symptomatic treatment with standard supplements or pills. When I experienced IBS or migraines, I examined mainly my food or attributed it to a vague diagnosis of being stressed. I did little to really observe myself on a daily basis to see what the connections were for me specifically or what the root causes might actually be.

This knowledge about myself, for myself, cannot be found in a textbook anywhere. It is different because it is information based on listening to myself—how my own body functions as well as how the environment impacts all different parts of me. It is understanding how I am interconnected together in my own unique way. In Ayurveda, we are all unique; therefore, these interconnections are specific to each of us. However, this does not mean that I disregarded scientific information from that point on. Rather, it was that I was balancing its importance in my life with the importance of listening to my Whole Self as well.

"Health is nothing more than being conscious."

—DR. SUNDARA, CHIEF PHYSICIAN & DIRECTOR AT MOUNTAIN TOP CLINIC

Listening to my internal environment to deepen my knowledge about myself is a form of consciousness. The body, mind, emotions, and soul are like guidance systems designed to tell us what is happening right now in the present moment. In other words, diseases or imbalances are also the gateways to becoming more conscious and aware.

I am fascinated by all of this exploration. Consciousness, or becoming more aware, is also experiential. This opportunity is available to everyone. It is not something reserved for an elite, scientific, or philosophical community. It is available to each of us in our everyday lives.

My health started to become less about first looking externally for understanding; instead, I began looking internally for the information that was already available if I took the time to listen. By listening, I began to notice the many disconnections in some very simple ways. For example, I noticed before some meals that I was not even hungry at all, usually when I was bloated or constipated. Yet, for some reason, I was extremely concerned about eating at every meal as I was convinced I would not have enough energy to do anything otherwise. There were a few reasons for this.

I grew up believing it was important to always eat three regular meals a day. I was listening to my mind telling me that I needed to follow this advice over my digestive system's message that I was not hungry. In addition, I often found it comforting to eat even though I knew my digestive system would not thank me for it later. I looked to food for comfort instead of where I really needed to comfort myself. I began to notice these disconnections everywhere. No wonder I felt so broken!

What started as simple daily observations about myself sowed the seeds to explore ever deeper rather than accepting surface-level explanations that did not resolve the underlying issues. Most of my life had been dominated by taking action to rectify a situation. If I had a problem, I wanted to know how to fix it, and then I busied myself with action. I believed in *making* things happen for myself. A couple of years later, I shifted away from this idea to a more balanced approach to life, which we shall explore further in chapter nine.

Listening to myself was an entirely different approach. It involved taking a step back to observe so I could understand the true nature of the situation first. In other words, to take time to listen to the root causes. At the time, I did not understand the far-reaching implications of this approach to life. Yet it formed the basis of all the exploration that was yet to come. In the meantime, as I studied Ayurveda, I began to apply the basic lifestyle principles that included a morning routine as well as adopting a diet that was appropriate to reduce my specific imbalances.

A huge benefit of studying while being a resident at MTC was that I could also observe the changes in the patients during their stay, some of whom have become good friends. One of these patients was Maria, whom I related to on many levels. I got to see the remarkable transformation in her and other patients. It was in seeing this for myself that convinced me to participate in the treatments as well at the end of my first stay.

***

Reflection

When I saw how little I listened to the most basic aspects of myself, I was shocked. I was soon to experience enormous benefits from listening because I began to notice the true nature of my situation. It was a deeper level of understanding of where I am right now, which had begun in chapter one. Consider:

- How well do you really listen to yourself? To your emotions? To your body? To your soul?
- Are there aspects where you believe you could benefit from listening better to yourself?
  - What are they?
- What simple metrics, similar to those I described for myself above, could you use to listen to these aspects of yourself?

If you are ready, make a note of at least a couple of these metrics each day, making the commitment to continue for a few weeks. The metrics I chose were simple and easy, and I noted them at the same time each day to remember them as part of my routine. After each week, review them. What do you notice about them?

At this point, my health was settling, but I still had few answers. I was to be continually disappointed and frustrated by this. Over the coming chapters, you will see it was no quick fix; it was a step-by-step process to recover my health. This was, at times, very frustrating. However, learning this gradually meant I could integrate changes into my life to make long-term, lasting improvements. It is precisely this lengthy journey that has made my life feel so rich today.

CHAPTER 4

Connections with the Whole of Me

"When I arrived at MTC I didn't want to live anymore," recalls Maria. I could relate to her as, despite having a new-found hope from Ayurveda, I was also still feeling exhausted with little desire to live. Maria's situation was more intense than mine. When I met Maria in September 2017, this was her second visit.

She first arrived at MTC in March 2017, having been bed-ridden for two years and barely able to walk because her feet throbbed so much. Maria described how it was as if her very bones were aching, and she struggled to breathe properly. Every part of her body was dry, including her nose, eyes, and throat and her digestion was very poor. Her immuno-globulin count (important antibodies to aid the destruction of viruses or bacteria) was extremely low, a measly count of two, whereas the normal count is fifty or more. Her health indexes also did not make any sense from a western point of view, as she was eating mostly vegetables, yet her cholesterol was high, and she barely slept.

I related to her in many ways.

Seeing the Whole Human

Prior to MTC, we both believed ourselves to have the ability to do everything at all hours of the day. Maria herself had been working extremely hard at two different jobs as a nutritionist, leaving the house at 6:30 a.m. and coming back at 11:30 p.m., thinking she could sustain this forever. Like me, she believed that if she focused on diet alone, then that was enough to ensure good health. In the past, we both had a firm belief in only paying attention to things proven by science. For most of our lives, we paid little regard to other aspects of ourselves, such as emotions and the nature of the mind or the soul.

Now, both Maria and I had come to MTC desperately seeking any alternative that would provide relief. On her first visit in March 2017, before we met, she told me she had arrived with a box full of papers from multiple tests, analyses, and examinations from different Spanish doctors; none of them could relieve her suffering despite all this scientific information. Maria told me one doctor even said she should forget about recovery and accept she would be bedridden for the rest of her days. She felt as if she wanted to die— since this did not feel like a life she wanted to endure much longer.

From her first time at MTC, her immunoglobulin improved by two counts, something the doctors back home had told her was not possible, and by the time I met her during her second visit, she was determined to get better.

She received a range of traditional Ayurveda treatments to initiate a reset that went on to support a full recovery. This included treatments such as Shirodhara, where medicated heated oil is continuously poured over the third eye located roughly in the center of the forehead. After this treatment, she usually found that she could sleep, something that had been eluding her for several years. Another treatment was Pizchail, an oil bath where warm medicated oil is poured over the body continuously. This helped her to relax and feel somehow warmed, grounded, and rebalanced.

Maria also received other targeted treatments such as Dharpanam, when lukewarm medicated ghee is squeezed gently over the eyes and held there with a dough-like substance padded around the eyes while the patient opens and closes their eyes. While this treatment did not sound appealing to me, she commented that it soothed her extremely dry eyes, so it felt good to her. She received a similar style of treatment for other parts of the body that felt dry.

I soon understood that the treatments at MTC were so much more than just going to the treatment room twice a day. For Maria, the treatments encompassing different parts of herself played a crucial role. Together we participated in daily yoga, meditation, and regular chanting. I enjoyed the chanting sessions with the other patients, and I found Maria's enthusiasm for these activities encouraging in my own journey as we both looked forward to these sessions immensely.

Reflecting later, we both remarked that in these sessions, we felt more connected, more Whole, somehow. Additionally, daily schedules were aligned to our natural body cycles; for example, eating the biggest meal at lunchtime when the digestive firepower is considered strongest. These were all activities that neither of us had considered important before, yet they brought a sense of happiness during our stay at MTC.

For Maria, these activities played a significant role in her recovery.

Dr. Sundara also spent time with each of his patients on a daily basis. For him, it is important to identify all the root causes, which extend to a patient's emotions, mental state, general lifestyle, habits, and environment back home. When I asked Maria about this, she commented that she found this aspect of her treatment extremely supportive, describing it as if her very soul was being treated. Dr. Sundara would tell her stories to help her see her illness or her approach to life from a different perspective.

Dr. Sundara said to me one day, half-jokingly, that he also played the role of psychologist as part of his physician activities. Shifting the perspective of the patients eases their emotional pain, calms thoughts, and connects patients back to their own souls in some way. It was the first truly holistic treatment I had ever observed.

"It is the duty of the physician to encourage the patient to be more and more conscious"

—DR. SUNDARA RAMAN, CHIEF PHYSICIAN AT MTC, INDIA

During her second visit in September 2017, when I met her, Maria looked better each day, and I was amazed at her transformation in only four short weeks. Toward the end of her stay, she came on a walk with the rest of the patients and me. Although I could see she struggled, she made it round our familiar loop through the tea plantation, something she simply had been unable to do when she first arrived. Her energy levels increased, her sleeping improved, her body felt nourished instead of dry, and she could breathe more easily. At the same time, her immunoglobulin had increased by ten counts at the end of her stay. Although Maria's health had improved tremendously, it took another year of continuing to follow the diet and lifestyle advice from MTC.

Finally, her immunoglobulin hit a count of fifty, which meant it was now in the normal range, her energy levels increased, and she was breathing normally. After this, she gradually returned to work as a nutritionist. However, now she includes in her treatments so much more than diet alone; she also considers the mind, body, and soul connections as well with her patients.

I could now see for myself the positive impact that was possible on people's lives when they are treated as a Whole Human—namely, the mind, body, and soul together as one connected being. In Maria's case, Ayurveda had the potential to support her chronic and complex illness because it started from the assumption that everything is connected, which meant everything was treated together as well.

Throughout my first stay at MTC, my own health symptoms were improved by acclimating to the Ayurveda schedules and routine. However, as Maria found, the recovery was very slow with only this support mechanism in place. I was finding the same. Although I felt a little better at MTC, I now decided to take the treatments myself; I wanted a renewed desire to live like the other patients that came and went from MTC.

Being Seen as Whole

At the end of my first stay of three months, in December 2017, I became a patient myself. As with other patients, medical tests were completed that showed I had a low white blood cell count. This explained why I kept getting frequent infections. I was also deficient in vitamin D, therefore highly likely to be deficient in other vitamins as well due to the poor digestive firepower of my stomach. I started on a holistic treatment program similar to Maria's that targeted the root causes behind my ill health.

One of the most drastic improvements in my health happened after the first seven days of treatment. For the first five days, I was prescribed medicated ghee, which is clarified butter that contains herbs specific to addressing the root causes behind my symptoms. The herbs are aimed at removing *Ama* from around the body as well as improving my weak digestion. I drank the medicated ghee in increasing amounts first thing each morning until the fifth day, where I drank around 140mL.

Each day I felt increasingly sick afterward with little energy, so I rested until lunch when the sickness eventually subsided. I shut off all electronics, lying on my bed watching the clouds go by outside. In the afternoons, I went for Swethenam—a steam bath to help sweat out *Ama* from the body. By the fifth day, I was feeling sick at the sight of the ghee, which in Ayurveda is a sign I had drank enough. On the morning of the sixth day, I took a strong, specially prescribed purgation medicine to eliminate all the *Ama* accumulated in the digestive system by the medicated ghee over the last five days.

Dr. Sundara told me not to worry and that I would start going to the toilet within a few minutes of taking the purgation medicine. Of course, I did worry. Though, I never understood why exactly, only that, by now, I understood worry was a habitual pattern that I had yet to change. A few hours later, I was in agony because I had not evacuated yet. It was as if my very cells were determinedly clinging to this *Ama*, resisting letting go. Sure enough, after a few hours, I started needing the toilet. Twenty-three times later, it was 3:00 a.m., and I felt thoroughly exhausted. However, a couple of days later, I could hardly believe the changes in how I felt.

It was as if a thick brain fog had lifted from around my head and eyes that I didn't even know had been there. I could think with clarity and ease. "*Is this how 'normal' people think*?" I wondered. When working, it had always felt like such a strain, but since it had always felt that way, I had never questioned it. I felt as if I came back down to earth, and everything seemed new to me, almost surreal. I was feeling present, in the now. Had I really been this disconnected? In the yoga sessions, I started to stretch in a way that hadn't been possible before; I could do shoulder stands, whereas previously, they brought on migraines if I attempted them. Had I really been that stiff? I felt so much calmer too. Had I really been in that heightened state of alertness my whole life?

I began to see the state I had been in, having previously thought it was normal. I was stunned at my own lack of awareness of how imbalanced my body, mind, and soul had been. It was at this point one crucial thing began to sink in about living: health is something to be experienced for myself. Our health—in other words, who we really are—cannot be understood just by studying intellectually. Despite learning basic Ayurveda principles around diet and lifestyle that I still apply in daily life today, it is this initial state of *experiencing* the benefits of good health that began to really motivate me to continue delving deeper.

I continued with Ayurvedic treatments for nearly three weeks before leaving MTC for the first time. During these three weeks, I also received Shirodhara occasionally; however, the majority of my treatments were Pizchail, the traditional Abhyanga, or full-body massages with medicated oils, and Podikizhi, when balls of heated, medicated powder are firmly pressed over the body repeatedly. Much like Maria, Dr. Sundara visited me daily to check how I was doing (and would adjust treatments accordingly), tell me stories, or offer advice about my situation.

Unlike other doctors, he took an interest in me from childhood to the present, in all aspects of my life: how I felt, where the anxiety had come from, underlying anger I felt, my lifestyle, friends, family, and general environment. He never dismissed anything I said as wrong, nor did I feel judged in any way, no matter what I said. His genuine concern and effort in supporting me were obvious in everything he said and did. In short, he listened to me.

As the treatment program continued, it was extremely comforting to feel seen, listened to, and supported in a holistic way. For the first time, I felt someone saw the Whole of me. If he saw me as naturally Whole, maybe I was not so broken after all? I wondered what life would be like if I truly saw the Whole of me the way Dr. Sundara did. It made me question the broken way I saw myself. Maybe I was not so broken after all.

The entire experience at MTC was the start of me questioning my life so far in a far deeper manner. Ayurveda is more than a healthcare system; it is an approach to life. This was sowing the seeds for the future direction my life would take. For the moment, however, I was more interested in my digestive issues, tiredness, migraines, and infections. I wanted to fully restore my own natural state of balance.

Medical tests were completed again at the end of my first stay, and they found both my white blood cell count and vitamin levels had returned to normal, indicating my digestive system had improved and was absorbing the nutrients I needed. Through the specialized combination of treatments unique to me, as well as the safe environment Dr. Sundara and his staff created at MTC, my health was slowly restoring. Completing these treatments had been like pressing a reset button on my life, putting down the foundations I needed to rebuild. Everything was beginning to feel more me, more Whole.

For the first time ever, I began to feel alive.

***

Reflection

MTC was the first time I experienced a holistically supportive environment. It led to a deeper questioning of the way I had lived to date, which had been in a disconnected way that was not supporting my health.

- Do you always live in a way that always supports your health?
    - In what ways is this not the case?
- Are there areas of your life where you think you are broken or disconnected in some way?
    - What are they?
- Think of someone who is supportive in your life. How do they perceive you?
    - What are the differences between this and how you perceive yourself?

In Ayurveda, while every individual is connected as part of a whole, we are also, at the same time, unique. Therefore, what is good health will be different between each of us.

- What is your own personal definition of good health?
- Have you considered all possible aspects of health?

Note that your own definition may change over time, and that is natural as you discover more throughout in life.

PART 3

INTERCONNECTIONS: FROM ISOLATION TO ONENESS

CHAPTER 5

Interconnections with Society

I'm going to rewind back to my teenage years for a moment.

At thirteen years old, I had one of the most painfully shocking experiences of my life. I writhed in seemingly unbearable pain on the bathroom floor until I vomited into the toilet bowl. It was so painful I thought death must surely be around the corner. But it was an entirely natural event for a woman.

It was my first period.

Having no idea what a period was supposed to feel like, I was shocked and in disbelief at the pain I'd endured. My second period was similarly agonizing. When I reached out for support, I received dismissive comments from family and teachers such as "you have to just get on with it" or "you have to get a job one day, you know, then what will you do?" Believing this to be the truth, I shut up and dealt with the pain. Fortunately, subsequent periods were more bearable, though I still suffered each month. I thought I was supposed to ignore the pain—it seemed to be the implied advice of everyone around me.

As soon as I was sixteen years old, I started taking the contraceptive pill, and I stayed on the pill for the next eighteen years. Contraceptive pills effectively prevented my period from happening naturally. After a month of studying at MTC, I started to think that this could be affecting my body coming back to a state of natural balance. It was another aspect of myself that was treated very differently at MTC. Dr. Sundara took a genuine interest in understanding my menstrual cycles. To date, I had largely ignored this aspect of being a woman as mostly inconvenient, often complaining about it with friends as per the cultural norm. As Dr. Sundara took this problem seriously, it led me to take it seriously as well.

It was another example where someone else seeing a part of me helped me to see more of myself.

Finally, after eighteen years, I decided to stop taking it before participating in the treatment program in December 2017. I had suppressed the screams of pain from my uterus for nearly two decades; it was now time to listen. Initially, I was extremely nervous to stop, but I was inspired by a friend who, six months earlier, had stopped taking the contraceptive pill after many years of having done so. She had had an erratic appetite for a long time, which meant she needed to eat every couple of hours yet could not understand why. When she ceased the contraceptive pill, not only did her periods return to normal quite quickly, but her appetite also changed almost immediately, so she no longer had this problem. Her fix seemed straightforward. As expressed in Ayurveda, everything is ultimately about coming back to a natural state of balance; menstruation is another natural cycle to align toward.

Since contraceptive pills prevented my period from happening naturally, I hoped that ceasing them might, as it had for my friend, help resolve at least some of my other challenges, such as digestive problems and migraines. However, when I returned for the second time to MTC in March 2018, I still had not had a natural period. It is difficult to describe the sensations. Though, for an approximation, I could say it felt as though the energy that was supposed to be released each month was building up inside me. It was as if my body was trying to remember what it was supposed to do naturally but could not seem to figure it out. It felt as if the energy was wrongly moving upward, which caused bloating, constipation, migraines, and increasing lethargy.

The pain was also a huge wake-up call on the consequences of not listening to my body or aligning to natural cycles in daily life.

Dr. Sundara advised me to go for a scan to make sure everything was alright physically. The doctor at the hospital in the local town examined me. The uterus lining was thicker than normal, which, if left to grow bigger, I was told could become a cancer risk. Other than this, there was nothing physically wrong with my uterus at all. The doctor said she would like to scrape out the lining. I had a decision to make.

Do I opt for the symptomatic treatment of scraping the lining, or do I attempt to identify and rectify the true underlying causes behind why my body was struggling to have a period? It was at this point I knew that symptomatic treatments were not enough for me anymore. I declined the option; I was determined to figure out the true causes instead.

When I arrived back at MTC, I stared out of my bedroom window at the thick, bleak mist that so often moved across the mountains. I could not even see any of the tree plantations that started right outside the premises. Silently and alone in my room now, I let the tears roll down my cheeks. I had work to do to connect back to my natural state of balance. This was the day I also accepted that there were things happening beyond what I could physically see, hear, smell, or touch. My body did not respond the same as my friend; it was yet another reminder that my body is unique and that I must find my own path.

In the meantime, I started to reflect more deeply on the connections between the influences of society and how I treated my body. Although this book is not about women's menstrual cycles, it is an example I believe is symptomatic of underlying issues with a modernized, western society. I had listened to other people's advice as well as followed cultural norms instead of listening to my own body. There was and still is a prevalent culture assuming that menstrual pain is normal and inevitable. Regular pain is indeed common. According to a 2012 study by Grandi G et al., 84.1 percent of women experience menstrual pain regularly, with 41.1 percent experiencing pain every cycle. Does pain being common really equal normal, or does it signify the scale of the issue? To me, pain is a signal something is wrong that wants attention, not that it is an inevitable, permanent part of everyday life where nothing can be done.

Additionally, my western doctor told me that IBS was something that had to be managed as there was no cure. Even the National Health Service in the United Kingdom states on their website that "there's no cure" and that "it's usually a lifelong problem." Why would I even seek to resolve the issue if I am being told I "just have to get on with it" or I am being told by health professionals it is a lifelong problem? In a study published in the online journal *Frontiers in Medicine* in 2021, Michael Jeitler et al. found that applying a personalized Ayurveda diet and lifestyle advice did indeed result in significant benefits to those suffering from IBS symptoms. They also found that the results were better than conventional, western, or nutritional therapy.

This led me into deeper questioning: How could such life-affecting assumptions have come to be taken as almost irrefutable facts of life? Although my IBS took another two years to resolve fully, the restoration of a normally functioning digestive system was not as irreversible as I had been led to believe. It is not that I am recommending Ayurveda as the only option or the best one for everybody. Rather, it is that there may be more options than we are being told are available, which can mean the difference between resolving the pain or living with it indefinitely.

Having seen the transformation in other patients in a variety of different instances for complex illnesses where a western approach has not helped, as well as experiencing a huge improvement in my own symptoms by the end of my time at MTC, I was convinced that suffering was not as inevitable as is often assumed. It is not that all illnesses are necessarily reversible, as even at MTC, there were cases where reversing a patient's causes was not always possible, and the focus was to ease the pain in a natural way instead.

Furthermore, at times I felt at odds with some of the yogic or Buddhist philosophy I studied at different ashrams or monasteries around the world, both before, in between, and after my time at MTC. I have also felt at odds with some of my mentors and guides over the years. While there is an underlying belief that we are all ultimately one connected being, almost all the practices I learned were focused on each of us going within to explore what was going on. The assumption is that when we change on the inside, it then changes our external environment. However, when it meant being out of alignment with cultural norms or assumptions implicit in society, it left me in a bit of a dilemma. It did not feel easy to pay attention to my own health or what I really wanted when the entire culture was different.

Health in the west tends to be something considered at an individual level. But now, I was starting to wonder whether we could benefit from considering health more at a societal or collective level as well. Is our health really that individual, or is it interconnected with others and the culture of society?

One person who understands these interconnections very well is Roslyn Snyder, an Australian psychologist with twenty-five years of experience. She treats many patients who are often considered the most challenging, including murderers, rapists, suicidal patients, or those who have been diagnosed differently multiple times, possibly having been transferred through multiple psychologists. She has a very different approach to most western psychologists today, as she incorporates ancient Aboriginal wisdom that we are one, wholly connected being.

She has even developed her own theory, called "Realm Theory," to explain the interconnections. She developed this theory so she could better understand how to treat her patients. Much of her work is around intergenerational trauma, which she has found often persists because there is a pattern of denial. She has sometimes found it challenging to work at an individual level, as when patients return home, they often go back into an unsupportive environment. For example, Roslyn told me she was treating one youngster who was feeling suffocated by her mother. When the youngster went back home, the mother simply denied this might be happening. What was the youngster supposed to do then?

She finds it much more effective to work at a "unit" level, whether the unit is a family or community. She told me that she worked with one community in Australia where domestic violence and sexual abuse within the families had continued for generations, with the entire town divided. If you were allied with one family, it was not allowed to connect with those allied to the other family. Violence was common between the two sides. No one remembered how it started other than there was an event about one hundred years prior, after which all inhabitants in the town either had to ally with one family or the other.

This divide extended into the prison system, where Roslyn initially went to help a group of twelve men in one of the prisons. Roslyn helped the prison inmates see the intergenerational connections and how said connections affected both their families and the entire community. The inmates understood that their circumstances could only change if they worked with the opposing side as well. So Roslyn worked with them and then finally brought both groups together to resolve their long-standing conflict. By the end, after a hundred years of conflict, the community could live in peace together.

From these discussions with Roslyn, I understood more about adverse childhood experiences (ACEs) where Dr. Robert Block, the former president of the American Academy of Paediatrics, is widely quoted as saying, "Adverse childhood experiences are the single greatest unaddressed public health threat facing our nation today." It is another example of how we are all interconnected; how we treat each other has a massive impact on our individual lives.

There have been numerous ACEs studies, which perhaps do not always get the attention they deserve, indicating that ACEs affect individual health. The first of these was by Kaiser-Permanente in California. It was one of the largest studies of its kind with nearly seventeen thousand participants, which found that around 67 percent of people experience one or more traumatic experiences in childhood, with 16.7 percent having four or more ACEs. It linked these experiences with chronic health problems, both mental and physical. They showed an increased risk of alcoholism, drug abuse, depression, suicide attempts, poor self-rated health, and a greater likelihood of severe obesity.

The greater the number of ACEs a person had, the greater the likelihood was that they suffered from some of the biggest health killers affecting the western world today, including ischemic heart disease, cancer, chronic lung disease, and liver disease. All of this has led me to wonder whether we need more options beyond individual care. In the entire self-development industry, there is a large focus on self-care.

Do we also need a focus on community care?

In other words, working together to resolve conflicts, no matter if they appear as individual symptoms of ill health or societal symptoms such as violence.

The impact of prevalent beliefs in society extends beyond symptoms of ill health. It affected my entire life choice, including my career. When I grew up, there was an assumption at school that I would go to university so I could get a city job, even though I knew deep down that was not really what I wanted to do. This implicit assumption had my best intentions at heart, but it was another way in which it overtook listening to what I actually wanted.

I felt even more at odds because I did benefit from the path I took; my university qualification opened the doors to me getting a well-paid job in the city. It was this financial backing that opened up further doors to go on my current journey. At this point, I still kept listening to family or friends back home asking unhelpful questions such as "when are you going to come back to reality?" It meant I continued to place emphasis on being productive or being seen to do something rather than taking a step back to really reflect.

It was nearly two years later that the snow globe shook again, affecting all different parts of my life, that I broke down yet again. This was when I shifted to really listen to what I wanted instead of what others were telling me I should do, as we shall further explore in chapter eight. In between these two years, it was like I was in a state of limbo, being resentful of this interference from others yet feeling like there was something I was still missing.

My continuing health challenges, along with the belief I could change my circumstances despite what many people said, kept me on a path to listen to ever closer to myself no matter where it led me. Initially, I was bitterly disappointed because I continued to experience debilitating pain while trying desperately to restore my natural menstrual cycle. It was precisely this frustration that would also lead me to an experiential understanding of the concepts of masculine and feminine energy.

As I left MTC for the second and final time in May 2018, I made my way to Dharamsala, home of the Dalai Lama, where there is a large Tibetan population and, therefore, Buddhism. During my stay, I participated in a silent retreat, where one twenty-minute meditation was so powerful it shattered any idea that I am, ever had been, or could ever be an independent individual in the way I had previously believed.

***

Reflection

From this painful experience, I learned there are often more options available than I was led to believe. For a long time, I did not really investigate what was underneath the surface-level symptoms, such as painful menstrual cycles, IBS, or migraines. However, I had found it was important to understand the nature of these interconnections; how our environment, family, and friends impact us and vice versa.

- Where in your life are you being told to "just get on with it"? Who are you listening to? Is it supporting you?
- What parts of your life are you going along with because it is what you have been told to do, even though it is not what you really want or is detrimental to your health?
- In contrast, where in your life do you notice positive connections around you that make you happy or maintain your health?

The better our interconnections are understood, the greater the potential for improving the health of an entire community, which includes you and me! As I came to see throughout my journey, we are all interconnected whether we like it or not. So it is not about whether we connect but rather about how we choose to connect with each other.

CHAPTER 6

We Are All Interdependent

As I sat down in the temple, at Tushita Monastery, Dharamsala making myself comfortable on my usual cushion, I prepared for another regular meditation. This meditation turned out to be an extraordinary meditation that I would remember for a long time to come. We were asked to sit in meditation, contemplating the next meal and everything that was needed to prepare it. Naturally, I thought about the food, starting with the rice.

The land was toiled by farmers, seeds sewn by farmers were then obtained, picked by laborers, transported in trucks that had been designed, manufactured, and bought in a whole different process, and then driven by truck drivers to a market. It was sold by a seller, bought by someone at the monastery, then received by staff to be washed and prepared by the kitchen staff. This was the same for every single ingredient. There were many vegetables or grains in each meal, and all the tools of the farmers and the production of the trucks were manufactured in different processes.

Next, I thought about the spoon and fork. The raw materials were mined in a whole entire process, then transported to the factory that was designed by architects, with machinery designed by engineers, then built by builders, with workers in the factory operating the machinery to finally produce the cutlery. Another truck, along with a driver, then transports this to a shop. The shopkeeper, in a building built by a whole different shop-building process, sells the goods to a buyer, and it is this buyer that brings them to the monastery to be used. It is also the same for the plates, tables, and chairs.

All of a sudden, twenty minutes was up, and I hadn't even gotten to recipes or cooking the food, or even the hire or retention of staff to actually cook the meal. I had also only considered the human connections making this flow of goods happen; I had not even gotten to our interdependencies with nature itself to grow crops or find raw materials. These huge, connected global networks, with entire processes, were all interconnecting together so I could have this one meal. There were so many people, with so much happening, that I could not even get part way through all the interdependencies in twenty minutes.

Wow.

I realized everything around me is interdependent, with networks everywhere, all somehow combining together in this thing called life. All together, all at once. I suddenly started to question this whole idea of "independence." Every single thing I did, right down to the basics of feeding myself one meal, depended on huge networks all interconnecting in an intricate ecosystem: chains upon chains of dependencies.

"The majority of people's problems are caused by the fact that they are disconnected with the rest of creation"

—*C.S. LEWIS*

It no longer made sense to think of myself, nor anyone else, as independent in the way I had been believing.

I now firmly believe that we are all interdependent on each other, as well as nature itself, whether we like it or not. A 2013 study by Matthew Lieberman titled "Social: Why Our Brains Are Wired to Connect" found that we are wired to coordinate together. It is when this connection breaks down, by instead engaging in activities that separate us, that the flow of life is interrupted. "We have a unique ability among species to "read" other people's minds, to figure out their hopes, fears, and motivations, allowing us to effectively coordinate our lives with one another," Lieberman explained.

I see it as if we have some intangible essence between us that means we can interconnect with each other. I started to marvel at how everything combines together so I can eat my one meal and that this happens every single meal throughout my entire life. How utterly beautiful!

Life is already intricately weaved together in one giant ecosystem. Sometimes it can be obvious to see that we are each dependent on each other to live, like when a person is physically dependent on others. It is less obvious when physically, we can navigate regular daily tasks ourselves. However, I had taken it for granted that all these things or people were there when I needed them, to the point where I believed I could therefore navigate my own life independently. It was yet another angle where I could now see why I had felt such confusion over the years. What an illusion for one to be in!

Now I understand that nothing is independent nor separated from anything else. We cannot ever disconnect from ourselves or others.

As I completed the silent retreat, on the one hand, I had more clarity that we are one interconnected humanity, yet on the other hand, I felt more confused because that did not seem to be the way life is lived in the west. So many activities common in society today stopped making sense. It is impossible to isolate people in the way so often done, for example, in our prison systems by locking up people. They are still connected to the rest of society, whether we like it or not.

As Roslyn showed in the last chapter, peace is brought about by integration, not isolation. Additionally, the idea of competition in the way so prevalent in markets today seemed at odds with our interconnectedness. We need each other, yet we try to outdo each other. Competition can be fun and exciting, but is it always friendly or in alignment with our interconnectedness? I started to wonder if this could be another reason why everything felt broken; as a society, we do not always act like one, Whole, integrated being.

***

Reflection

Simply seeing how we are interconnected at a practical level completely changed my entire outlook on life, including my approach to business, communities, and friends.

- In what ways do our interconnections affect how you see our relationships with each other?
- How could approaching life as a journey in companionship with others change the very fabric of society itself?
- What does "the flow of life" mean to you?

CHAPTER 7

Feminine and Masculine Connections

One morning in my hotel room in India, shortly after leaving MTC for the second and final time, I collapsed on the bathroom floor sobbing intensely, with an enormous sense of relief; the signs of my first natural period in eighteen years had arrived. I was overjoyed. My body was beginning to remember how it functions. I naively thought my menstrual cycles would quickly return to a normal, healthy pattern, but again, I was very wrong.

Instead, it marked the start of a journey going ever deeper into different parts of myself to understand the true causes of the struggles behind my menstrual cycles, which went way beyond looking at the physical parts of my body. After leaving MTC, despite knowing that the pain I was experiencing was not related to any physical signs, I still thought that if I just kept following the Ayurveda diet and lifestyle advice, everything would naturally sort itself out.

I adopted a more Ayurvedic lifestyle; I followed a self-care morning routine that included many aspects advised in Ayurveda texts. I got up at a regular time each day and followed specific advice such as tongue scraping, application of nasal oil, and facial massage, which was followed by yoga practice and then meditation. I ate a plate of fruits, allowing time for it to digest (in Ayurveda, fruits are not meant to be eaten with other foods), and I ate a more filling breakfast later. My main meal was at lunch, a light evening meal would follow it, and then I went to bed at the same time each night.

As much as I could while traveling, I followed Ayurveda eating guidelines for my specific Prakruti, or body constitution, and other Ayurveda advice to reduce my Vikruti, or imbalance. I was convinced if I stayed on the path of following these yogic and Ayurvedic principles, then the challenges around my cycles would sort themselves out eventually.

I kept learning more in the hope of becoming better able to cope in daily life. For the remainder of my time in India, I spent time learning more about yogic and Buddhist philosophies in Dharamsala, where I experienced the life-altering meditation in the previous chapter. I left India in July 2018 to return to Spain. I also studied yoga therapy in between the residential stays at MTC, and I applied all this knowledge to teach yoga, meditation, and basic Ayurveda at a retreat in Andalucia in southern Spain. Around this time, I traveled to different farms or other yoga retreats in Spain to volunteer.

My energy levels, although improving, still remained low with my digestion erratic, and I continued to have regular migraines. My menstrual cycles were also not returning to normal. I had about ten days feeling fine before it all went downhill with bloating, constipation, and mood swings, which intensified daily until my period actually came. All my physical symptoms magnified until the release came with my period. I frequently broke down in tears or felt angry for no identifiable reason close to my period, so I would often stay in my room to avoid people during this time. It could be up to ten days late, during which time I found it almost impossible to function, only I kept trying to continue because I did not know what more I was supposed to do.

Surely better habits were supposed to equal better health. If I followed the routines, then everything would sort itself out, right?

Despite persisting for a year and a half, this approach had not resulted in the desired results of feeling healthy, happy, or Whole. Something different was needed. I thought if I changed my environment yet again, that might help. So I decided to move to Bali, where there is a thriving digital nomad scene. I hoped to get inspired support from others who had successfully made the switch to living the life of a digital nomad, which was something I desired too. Bali is also well-known for the spiritual side of life, so I hoped to get some insight there. Only by the time I arrived, I couldn't really concentrate on anything. With a maximum of about ten days of feeling good enough to work each month before the downward period cycle began again, it was hard to achieve much. I kept trying to continue; only I simply felt frustrated at the lack of progress.

Finally, it got to a point one month in Bali, where I was fifteen days late for my period. It was as if the snow globe was now being shaken nonstop, forcing me to listen. I was in so much physical pain it was unbearable, and I had a migraine that lasted for days. I was hyperventilating into panic attacks, breaking down in tears, and feeling so much rage it was as if I wanted to destroy myself somehow; I felt like a broken pressure cooker. I was trying so hard to change my life, yet I could not get a handle on this most basic aspect of living for a woman.

I felt like a failure.

I could not help the feeling that I was somehow "missing" something. Furthermore, I felt that I was "missing" some feminine aspect that was needed to help regulate my cycles. I did not know how to explain this to people in words. It was something I felt intuitively. I had been reluctant to pay much attention to this idea of the feminine, despite discussions like this being common in a place like Bali. However, I was so desperate that I was willing to consider any alternative options.

Finally, I wondered if a Reiki healer might be able to help me, so I found one in Bali who came highly recommended and went there straight away. I told her what was wrong. At the time, I had no idea what I was saying. Yet she seemed to understand and told me to set the intention to bring in the feminine energy throughout the session. She let me know that she could not guarantee it would regulate my menstrual cycles, although I had a funny feeling this session was going to help me. Reiki healers typically work by realigning and unblocking energy centers so that our energies flow better.

I did not realize how much this one session would change my life.

Throughout the session, I was almost pleading with the universe to bring in the feminine part of me so I could feel Whole and have a period. At the end of the session, the healer told me to go and look in the mirror. I looked at the girl staring back at me; my eyes were wide and bright, and my face looked different somehow, more alive. I felt more Whole. She said she could feel my strong intention to bring in the feminine energy, and that part had now come back into my body.

I truly felt as if a part of me had come home. Initially, it felt as if there were two voices in my head, which was extremely disconcerting. It was as if this new resident, the feminine energy, had moved in to unsettle the ways of the long-time resident, the masculine energy. It's a weird feeling that is difficult to describe, but then the most amazing thing happened the very next day: my period came.

I was delighted, almost to the point of deliriousness. Since my visit to the Reiki Healer, almost every menstrual cycle became regular to the exact day. Over the coming months, the ratio of good days to bad days increased steadily, and the bad days also became less severe. This event set me on a journey to listen ever deeper to the pain I experienced each month—as if it was some sort of gauge as to how well I have listened to myself in general over the previous month.

As the shaking of the snow globe subsided, a different version of me settled in again. In the weeks after visiting the Reiki healer, the feeling that there were now two parts of me gradually subsided as I felt more Whole, more complete. This is the type of experience that is almost impossible to describe in words or verbally communicate to others. It is again something that has to be experienced; this, to me, was another example of *real knowledge*. From this one session, I felt as though I had been given the gift of a new life. It was crazy, yet it was also the one thing that brought me lasting relief after a year and a half of agony.

I still almost cry every time my period arrives because I am so grateful for it; the pain of being disconnected from this natural cycle has helped me to appreciate the importance as well as experience the joy of being reconnected with it. More broadly, it changed my perspective on all natural cycles; the price to pay for ignoring them is interminable suffering, whereas the reward for aligning to them is good health. It took me a while afterward for the impact of this new presence of feminine energy to really integrate.

Eventually, I would see another angle of the difference between feminine and masculine energies, which we will discuss in a later chapter. It also triggered deeper reflection not only with respect to my own masculine and feminine energies but also the interconnections this has with society as well.

The Feminine and Masculine Energies

Throughout many conversations and reflections, some distinctions gradually became clearer to me. There is a common mix-up in society between "identifying as female" and "the feminine energy." Whether we identify as a man, woman, or nonbinary is a matter of biology—there are definable physical differences. My own biology is pretty clear; I identify as a woman. This is different from the qualitative, nonphysical feminine energy.

In the popular Chinese "taiji," or yin-yang symbol, the yin represents feminine energy. It is commonly understood to relate to darkness, the moon, cold, emotions, or anything related to receiving, allowing, or *being*. To me, the characteristics of feminine energy are nurturing, sensitivity, supportiveness, gentleness, tact, intuition, and cooperation. The Chinese yang, or masculine energy, relates to lightness, the sun, heat, or anything related to giving, moving, or *action*. Typical masculine energy characteristics are assertiveness, logic and analysis. The taiji symbol integrates as one; both are needed to balance in Wholeness or oneness.

As I came to understand these different energies, I could see that I had been led largely by the masculine energy throughout my life. I had a very strong belief in taking action to make things happen for myself: new job roles, moving companies, or changing locations. I kept pushing, hardly ever resting unless my physical body started shutting down. Rarely did I step into the feminine energy to take a step back, reflect, and allow or let things happen for me; when I grew up, this approach was synonymous with laziness.

I was hardly ever gentle with myself; I neither acted in a way that genuinely supported me, nor did I pay much attention to nurturing my body. The expectation where I worked was often to work long hours, particularly when there were last-minute "emergencies." Yet I was not exactly working in the emergency services; I worked in back-office departments far removed from anything representing mortal danger. It was as if relaxation time was treated as a luxury, not a necessity or a priority. Here, it is again possible to see the influence of society on how I lived my life; I never questioned this expectation. I thought I had to "just get on with it" again.

I denied a role for intuition, the feminine energy. In earlier chapters, I already mentioned the dominance of logic or rational science in my life to the exclusion of anything else. When I grew up, I thought contemplation was something approached from an entirely analytical, logical perspective, in other words, a masculine perspective—not at an intuitive level or a feminine perspective that *feels* its way through a problem.

In summary, I was a woman dominated by masculine energy, with an underrepresentation of feminine energy. I had no awareness this was happening. Feminine energy had a less-than-equal status to masculine energy in my life, though I had not seen it in these terms until now. It just so happened that this imbalance showed up as physical pain in my uterus. Although this might not be the case for every woman experiencing menstrual pain, for me, it was a part of my body that needed more feminine energy to function smoothly.

In contrast, I have several male friends who have expressed to me the challenges they faced growing up as they naturally possessed a lot of feminine energy, but it was not alright to express it. One male friend even attempted suicide over this. Yet here I was, a woman, facing exactly the same challenge!

It seemed to me that expressing our natural feminine energy has little to do with what gender we are. We all possess both energies, although the balance between these, like everything, will be different between different people. Its expression has more to do with its acceptability in society. Again, I saw the impact that the general values of society have on living our individual lives.

I do not know if I will ever be certain exactly why this part of my body decided to scream in pain, only that it helped me learn the distinction between identifying biologically as a woman and the feminine energy. In the meantime, I was not out of the woods. IBS symptoms, migraines, and general lethargy persisted, although markedly less severe than prior to my visit to the Reiki Healer. I was also disappointingly lacking in direction in life, as my attempts to design a digital nomad life in Bali had not worked.

While living there, I met an American man. Eventually, we decided to move to Vietnam in November 2019. Wanting to live in a cooler place, we settled in a quaint hill town called Da Lat. It was there that yet more of my beliefs to date would crumble, along with an increasing experiential understanding of the importance of both feminine and masculine energies for a balanced life.

This was another deeper layer that brought me a few steps closer to finding peace within myself.

***

Reflection

This distinction between masculine or feminine energies as well as versus male or female was an extremely useful distinction to help me understand some of the confusion I had felt throughout my life.

- Are there examples in your life where the feminine energy is getting mixed up with being female, or the masculine energy is getting mixed up with being male?
  - Examples such as work, family, friends, or your culture generally? How is this impacting the flow of life?
- Given the definitions of masculine and feminine energies cited above, which energy dominates your life?
  - Conversely, which energy is underrepresented?
- What is a healthy, natural balance point between masculine and feminine energies for you?

PART 4

SEEING THE GAP: FROM SUFFERING TO FREEDOM

CHAPTER 8

Move into Space

"What do you see in this temple?" one of the nuns at Thosalming nunnery in Dharamsala asked. I was participating in a retreat there shortly before leaving India. Our group proceeded to point out all the objects in the room: the stools, meditation cushions, rugs, alter, flowers, paintings, the list went on.

Then she asked, "What about the space? Look around. Isn't that actually most of what is here?" We all sat in silence. My gaze drifted around the room. So much space! "If it wasn't for the space, you would not even see the objects," she summed up. I sat there absorbing this information. I was so fixated on objects; now, suddenly, I could see so much space between the objects that I had not seen before.

The space has always been there. I was just not aware of it.

Up until now, I had not given space much consideration because it does not exactly *do* much, and for most of my life, I had only really considered objects. In Ayurveda, Akasha is one of the five elements. Exact translations are difficult;

however, it roughly translates to "space"" or "atmosphere." It is this element that allows all the other elements to function; Apus (air) needs space to move through, Agni (fire) needs space to burn, Apas (water) water needs space to flow into, and Prithvi (earth) needs space in which to settle. It is a very large part of Wholeness or the oneness of the universe.

Space has come to mean more to me than merely being the emptiness that allows the elements to function. Additionally, it is what provides the context for everything that happens in life. As an example, space is also the gap between a situation and the actions I take as a result. Victor Frankl, the author of *Man's Search for Meaning*, describes this as the gap between stimulus and response. The stimulus is the situation in the present moment, whether it is a pleasant or unpleasant experience. The response is the action that I will decide to take as a result of the stimulus. The gap is the space that allows for new insight, questions, or ideas.

Victor Frankl is an extreme example of how powerful this space can be; it was how he distanced himself from the dreadful conditions of a concentration camp. Instead of being caught up in the experience of the dreadful conditions of the concentration camp, in this gap, he could choose his response to the stimulus rather than be caught up in the pain of it all. For Victor, this was how he escaped the pain to find freedom from the extreme suffering all around him.

I really admire Victor's strength and courage. From my own experience were many times when moving into this gap did not seem possible, and my circumstances have not been nearly as severe as Victor's. After leaving MTC, there were days when I was in so much pain from either IBS or my menstrual cycles that all I could do was "batten down the hatches," cry, and attempt to keep breathing until the pain eventually subsided.

In times like this, symptomatic relief can be helpful; this in itself can provide the space needed to initiate a long-term shift. However, here is the point with symptomatic relief I believe often gets missed; it is what provides the space to be able to identify the root causes of suffering, whereas, in much of modern western life, symptomatic relief seems to be the endpoint. It takes the place of looking deeper into what is really going on or moving into a space to allow something new to come in.

Until I started to move into different spaces, I often got too caught up in the "stimulus and response." On a couple of occasions in my twenties, if I became really upset by a situation, I stopped eating much, sometimes for months. From listening more to myself, I became aware that I could dive into extremely depressive moods for days yet be unable to identify why, nor could I shift this feeling. During this time, I felt powerless, like a victim of circumstance, lacking hope and wondering, "What was the point in life when I feel this bad?"

Eventually, the feeling always shifted, but I did not know when it would happen nor how exactly; I did not have mechanisms for navigating through this. In learning to be able to move into space in different ways, it meant I could learn to shift feelings. I could change my circumstance. I was not powerless as I believed for most of my life.

There are endless types of spaces. It could be something as simple as taking five minutes to focus on breathing or sitting quietly for fifteen minutes contemplating a matter with hands around a comforting mug of coffee. Contemplative meditations are a popular form of space from which to see things differently.

As I came to experience after leaving MTC, space allows many different insights to come in. The continued suffering was a signal of underlying misalignments in my life. In the next section, I will share a few of the most important ways moving into a particular space opened up opportunities to be more Whole and more me, which in turn meant I could step toward freedom from suffering.

When I pressed the pause button later in January of 2020, it created a gap to allow new inspiration to come in. I moved into a gap that focused on happiness by reflecting on who I really am and what I really want. Zooming out then allowed me to be in a space where I could observe my emotions instead of getting caught up in them. This brought a sense of freedom because I could see the underlying reasons behind my behavior. Noticing my thoughts yet not believing them as absolute truth meant I could shift into a space that allowed me to distance myself from the mind chatter. I realized that things are not always exactly as the narrative of the mind leads me to believe, and coming from a space of unconditional love is what really brought in a sense of unity.

All these experiences combined to radically change my perspective on living life, and we will discuss these experiences in further detail in the upcoming chapters.

***

Reflection

What I learned in the following chapters was how I often caused my own suffering by being too caught up in the experience, unable to step away to see with clarity. It led to a feeling of powerlessness or as if I was a victim of circumstance, with no choice in how to respond.

- Can you already notice areas of your life or specific situations where you feel powerless? Or that you are a victim of circumstance?
  - Remember, everything is interconnected. How could this be impacting your current health? Future health?
  - How could this be impacting other people? The environment?
- Look around you. What percentage of what you see in front of you is space, and what percentage of it is solid or liquid matter?

CHAPTER 9

Balancing Doing & Being

In January 2020, I got to another extremely low point. I was heartbroken because a relationship ended with a man I cared for deeply. I was mind-broken, as all the things I had done to start a small business had not worked out, and body-broken, as my digestive system had once again stopped functioning properly. I finally pressed the pause button.

The fairy tale life I had imagined was well and truly smashed.

Prior to this, as my boyfriend and I settled in Vietnam, I was delighted at what first seemed to be a fairy-tale romance. However, over the next month, it was clear this romantic connection was not going to last. We were barely talking to each other at this point, yet I did not want to let him go; I did not want to be alone, in turned out the relationship wasn't alleviating this persistent feeling of loneliness.

It was also becoming clear my latest idea of becoming an Ayurveda lifestyle mentor was not going to work, but I did not know what else to do, so I kept working at it. During this time, my IBS symptoms flared again, along with severe headaches.

By Christmas 2019, my digestive system was so bad I began a cleanse with simple Ayurvedic remedies. I was absolutely desperate to keep going, keep doing, keep moving, to avoid my life falling apart completely; I was desperately trying to avoid the inevitable.

Rewinding to my early years, I had followed the path I thought I was supposed to bring happiness and contentment. I was told it was important to get good grades in school, so I did. I was told it was important to go to a good university and get good grades, so I did. I was told it was important to find a stable career path out there in the marketplace, so I did. I became a chartered accountant even though I did not like it at all. I was told it opened up more opportunities if I worked in big global companies, so I worked in the world's biggest banks in London. I believed working hard meant you were more valuable to a company, so I worked harder to be of more value. I slogged away at all of this, believing that was what life looked like.

I often joked about getting F.O.M.O (Fear of Missing Out) as I found it hard to say no at work or when asked to go out with friends. I treated it as a joke, ignoring the signals that something was not aligned in my life, that I was disconnected in some way. All along, I was hiding the suicidal feelings, trying to carry on with life as if those feelings were not there.

Even at MTC, more than one year after leaving London, I still felt a need to keep doing. I participated in all the activities as well as my classes, plus studying outside of class. To make the most of my time there, I was still caught in the belief that this meant doing more. By this time, I had at least realized I was in a weakened physical state, but I did not stop. When I left, I still continued with this idea of needing to keep "doing." I needed to keep achieving tangible things; otherwise, what value did I have? I was desperate to figure out what I would do instead.

I felt I was lacking in some way without a clearly identifiable career, so I decided more doing was needed.

When I moved to Spain in 2018, as well as volunteering on farms or yoga retreats, I attempted to build a travel website. I soon realized it did not make sense if I did not intend to continue traveling, so it morphed into a self-help website instead. It was exhausting trying to do both things at once.

Then, in Bali, I thought I might start as an Ayurveda lifestyle mentor. Every second digital nomad in Bali seemed to be a coach of some sort, so I thought I would follow them. By the time I got to Vietnam, I was working hard on this latest idea. This idea also never got off the ground. I kept slogging away, not giving myself space to pause because all I knew how to do was keep "doing."

So. Much. Doing.

I was exhausted!

Finally, in January 2020, this belief in relentless "doing" shattered completely. The inevitable happened. The fairy-tale travel romance I had created in my head had not matched with reality, and my then-boyfriend split up with me and left Da Lat. I was too distraught to do anything at all. No amount of external relationships, friends, or work had shifted this lonely, disconnected feeling I had.

I knew it was time to face this now. All this time, I had been avoiding looking internally at the connections I did not have with myself. At long last, I was out of all "doing" options.

Finally, I paused.

There was nothing more I could think of to do. My entire life, I had not been asking the right question in the first place. The question I had been asking was, "What is the matter?" and then trying to find solutions to it. This had not been the most supportive question to ask. The question to ask was, "What matters to me?" and then to take aligned action in accordance with the answer.

There is a huge difference between these two questions. The first externalizes the situation. In other words, it looks at what seems to be wrong at the surface level, which was then followed by attempts to fix the world around me in the form of career, geographical location, or relationships with others. Even leaving my entire world behind in London had not shifted this perspective on life.

The internalized question focuses inward, to listen to the heart, or inner guidance, to identify the true underlying causes of discontent and also what I actually want. I was feeling lonely, so the external solution seemed to be I needed to be in a relationship or build new friendships. The internalized solution was to look at my relationship with myself to see where I was disconnected.

I felt as if I did not have value in the world, so the external solution seemed to be to identify goals to achieve in the form of qualifications or job titles. The internalized solution was to look at why I believed I did not have value as a human being in the first place. My digestive system was in pain again, so the solution seemed to be a cleanse. Although this did relieve the symptoms in the short term, I was still not looking deep enough internally at the inner mental, emotional, or soul disturbances.

To look internally, I needed to take a step back and give myself the space to reevaluate my current situation. As Julia Cameron comments in her book *The Artist's Way*, "*A closet stuffed with ratty old clothes does not invite new ones. A house overflowing with odds and ends and tidbits you've held on to for someday has no space for the things that might truly enhance one day.*"

I was now ready to let go of all the doing that had not been supporting me, similar to throwing out the old, to make space for something new.

For the next couple of months, I barely touched my laptop. I spent time alone contemplating, drawing, or out in nature, and I shifted my focus to reflect on my life to date; what had worked, what had not worked (which was most things), and why they had not worked. Instead of listening to other people or even to the chattering of my own mind telling me I needed to keep on doing, I shifted my focus to receive information from my own inner guidance system that had been there all along. My own intuition. From this space, I realized I did want to identify a purpose, but that it needed to come from within me, from what brought me joy in life.

Synchronistically, the support I needed appeared at the right moment. My friend Janet, a purpose mentor, has a unique method for healing trauma through her program, The 5th Door. She is an ex-advertising creative who, in her words, "swapped promoting consumer brands for elevating the human brand" and cleverly uses language to help go beyond the surface to look at who we really are, as well as who we are not.

She was about to run a workshop that guides people through exactly my challenge. In a previous workshop also run by Janet, we used her own specially developed techniques to uncover our limiting beliefs, then turned these around to be lessons for us in our lives. I participated in this workshop in Bali, where it had been a big first step in understanding myself better. The second workshop went further to build on these lessons, which guided me to determine what I care about, what drives me, and what I really wanted to do in life. It was practical, yet it went deep into ourselves through different exercises to understand this—the context around my purpose.

It did not matter what this purpose turned out to be, only that it had come from somewhere inside me. I realized I enjoyed many aspects of my roles in banking, such as the complex global analyses, ensuring processes and system functions, as well as the project style of working. Only, I did not want to do this in banking anymore. I wanted to do this with companies that focused on well-being or learning. I did not want to work alone; after all, I wanted to work in a team with other people toward a shared vision. I wanted to be part of a community that creates realistic opportunities for us to live our lives in a space of contentment and good health.

As I completed the second workshop, I left with a new spring in my step, feeling hopeful. Finally, I was getting the clarity I had been seeking in my life. I now began realigning myself to launch into what I truly felt I was supposed to be doing. I had no idea how I was going to find this new job, but something inside me now intuitively knew it was all going to work out.

I started to connect with different people online. Not pushing anything but focusing on establishing genuine connections with others. Sure enough, a couple of months later, I had not one, but two jobs; one in the fitness industry and one in well-being, doing exactly the type of things I love to do. This immense shift happened when I was ready to let go of what I already knew was not working, create space to allow in what I actually wanted to attract, step into the unknown, and trust that it would work itself out.

This internal approach of looking at myself as the Whole Human was a completely different way to decide what to do with my life than what I had previously known. I was searching internally to identify my own unique life purpose and, therefore, my life direction. This felt so natural, so in alignment with who I am naturally. It started by asking the question, "What is it I truly want?"

This approach has so many implications for the way we live our lives today.

I was beginning to understand that coming back to a place of balance—and thus, good health—was less about the "how to" guides around changing behavior and more about moving into a space to allow the change to happen naturally. It is also the awareness with which this is done. The space is where I could take notice of the deep inner guidance coming through so that I was open to seeing new opportunities.

In the closing chapters of her book *Just a Thought: A No-Willpower Approach to Overcome Self-Doubt & Make Peace with Your Mind*, Dr. Amy Johnson notes, "Most self-help books are full of behavioral change but I would argue that those behaviors aren't what led to the author's change—insight did." This has a wide societal impact because much of western society currently focuses on behavioral change, like taking action, completely missing the insight needed first. Amy has worked with many people facing anxieties or addictions and consistently found that what creates lasting change is not obsessing over behavior but rather in first seeing things differently, so the behavior changes naturally.

One morning, I was in conversation with Ela, a friend whom I met online. She is a women's leadership coach and life coach specializing in supporting women to recognize their potential in both career and personal life. When we met initially, she offered a complimentary session where she guided me to look beyond my emotions, which I consider to be another kind of surface-level symptom, toward recognizing underlying behavior patterns. This triggered yet another huge shift in my life that I will share in the next chapter.

As we chatted, she told me she has found time and again that seemingly successful executive women, driven for decades by external achievements, usually come to her when they are not experiencing the well-being or happiness they had hoped. Ela supports them to rebalance their life by creating spaces to breathe within their daily life and to review what is happening. She finds this has a huge impact on her clients in all areas of their life, from their relationships with themselves, with others, and communication in general, while also positively shifting their attitude toward work—another example of how life is all connected together.

Ela also mentioned multiple physical symptoms with her clients that tend to reduce themselves naturally as she works alongside them, from being overweight to diabetes. As we discussed this, I noted that often this type of life-improving rebalance does not necessarily require a long pause like me; it can happen gradually within the current environment, inclusive of—and not in place of—everyday life.

"It's not what you're doing, it's your energetic state of awareness. A busy mind does not leave any space for inspiration to come in. It's too busy to notice."

—JEY MATTHEWS, INTUITIVE CHANNELLER & SPIRITUAL ACTIVATOR

My entire life had been so busy with "doing" that I had not taken the time to really, truly, deeply reflect on this question.

I do not know whether inspiration was trying to come through all my life or not. I would have been too busy to notice anyway! When I reflected on this a couple of years later, I came to see this pause as similar to the feminine energy, which to me is a state of awareness that is open to actively receiving information from any source. The masculine energy drives "doing." For my whole life, I had been unwittingly driven by the masculine energy as if action was the starting point for healthy change in life.

My career had centered around implementing or improving processes and systems, as if this was the goal in itself, with little attention paid to whether this action was actually what was needed. I had been missing a crucial understanding that contributed to feeling so imbalanced in daily life; I had never allowed myself to sit in this feminine state of *awareness*, only to move into the masculine state of *doing*. It was in allowing both types of energies that brought me to a place of contentment with the direction of my career. It enabled me to naturally come back to my own unique place of balance, not a place defined by someone else or society. It further meant I could now bring my whole self to work, something I had never felt I was able to do until now.

Then the COVID-19 pandemic hit, with countries shutting down their borders in March 2020, including Vietnam. I decided to remain here rather than go back home to a way of life I could not make sense of anymore, and my personal journey continued.

My next powerful lesson shifted me further along my path by learning the importance of listening to another part of myself: my emotions.

***

Reflection

I thought reflective activities had to be serious, and I spent a lot of time on such activities— days practicing meditation or yoga at ashrams and monasteries throughout the world. Now I value any activity that genuinely brings me joy because it is in being in the moment and enjoying life that somehow makes space for pivotal insights to come in. Up until now, I had felt guilty if I enjoyed life, but now I saw the necessity of it. It means I can get those insights to support not only myself but also humanity at the same time.

- What is your balance like between your reflective and fun activities and "doing life" activities?
- How good are you at taking the time to do something not to achieve anything in particular but rather to enjoy doing it?
  - If you want to do more of it, how could you do this?
  - Remember, even five minutes of joy can change your outlook on your entire day.
- What matters to you?
- What is it you truly want?

CHAPTER 10

Emotions Are Signposts

"I want to hang myself."

I looked around my temporary flat in Hanoi, where I had just moved after six weeks in Nha Trang. *"The ceiling bar in this flat will support my weight. I can get a rope. I don't want to live!"* This might sound extreme to you, yet these types of thoughts were common for me. Throughout my life, I often got to the point where my emotions were so intense I did not know what to do with them.

Caught up in the moment without understanding how to handle these emotions, seemingly extreme thoughts or actions would suddenly seem totally rational.

In my late teens and early twenties, self-harm seemed rational in the moment. Throwing tantrums in front of a boyfriend when I was upset by his actions seemed like an obvious reaction in order to get his attention. My inability to understand or even properly acknowledge my emotional state manifested in many ways like this. It was often followed by embarrassment at my actions as I tried to mend relationships I had broken. This was a repeated pattern of behavior; I would know how I was reacting was unkind, yet I felt as though I could not control it.

I do not believe people, including myself, act in an unkind way because we are "just bad." There is something unseen or not being acknowledged underlying this. I was about to find out what that something was.

Since leaving London four and a half years ago, I was still at a loss to understand why I had really left. I was completely frustrated with myself. If one more person told me to practice a "peace and love meditation," read some affirmations, write in my journal, or practice some breathing exercises, I think I could have punched them in the face. I was doing many supportive activities as part of my daily habits, yet nothing shifted these inner critical voices telling me things like: *"You're useless!" or "Who do you think you are, running round the world like this? Put up with your pain and go back to your old job!"* or *"See, I told you, nothing ever changes. Same old pain, you can't escape it!"*

A big breakthrough in understanding why these voices were so persistent came at this point where I wanted to hang myself. Once again, it was from the depths of the now all-too-familiar phrase: *"I can't go on like this. I don't know what to do!"*

The mountains in Da Lat had been a safe, insulated place while much of the world was focused on the COVID-19 pandemic. As there were no cases of COVID-19 in Da Lat, life continued more freely than in many parts of the world.

However, my time there was coming to a close, so I moved to Nha Trang, along the coast of Vietnam. Then, after Nha Trang, my heart broke all over again, this time in a different way with a soul friend. From our first connection online, I felt as though there was something different with him—something more intense.

The close friendship began a couple of months before when I met this soon-to-be-close friend. It was an instantaneously close connection that developed despite him living in California while I was in Vietnam. It was an exciting, soul-deep connection I had never experienced before. It felt so good to be connected in a deep way with someone after feeling so lonely for so long.

Soon, I was enmeshed in an intense friendship with regular contact via text, voice, and video calls. It was one of the most intense yet exhilarating few weeks of my life. I finally felt connected to someone in a deeper soul-level way I could not explain. Yet after a few weeks, I started to notice I felt completely drained after we spoke, to the point where I had to sleep for an hour after our calls together. Throughout this time, there were elements of our dynamic I wasn't comfortable with either. I attempted to raise it with him on a couple of occasions, but he dismissed my concerns, so I ignored them. This was the first time I had ever felt such a deep connection with anyone, so I was not going to ruin it by creating problems.

I was desperate to keep hold of this connection no matter what, as the alternative was to go back to feeling lonely again. That was not going to happen, I decided.

During another intense phone call, he suddenly said I must be tired and hung up on me. He had sounded high throughout the call and wasn't making much sense, which I ignored because I really wanted to talk with him. This time the chaotic extreme feelings that came up after the call were so intense I did not know what to do with them. All I knew at that point was something was really off, so I had to say something. I was still, at this point, not particularly good at expressing myself in a kind, honest way. The snow globe was about to be violently shaken again.

Two days later, I texted him, saying I wanted nothing to do with his business, which I had previously offered to help him with. He bit back, saying he wanted nothing more to do with me at all. That, apparently, was that. I felt totally abandoned. How could he not see that I needed him? It was at this point I completely broke down, feeling surrounded by clouds of dark despair. I was angry because it was another habitual outburst from me but also confused because I had felt as if I could not help myself.

Deep down, I knew I was never going to actually end my life, even though these extreme thoughts and emotions were common. I had become very good at "pulling myself together" to pretend everything was alright over the years. An hour later, I buried my emotional state and went with an estate agent to look for a flat in Hanoi, chatting away enthusiastically about how much I was enjoying my time in Vietnam.

However, there was a difference when I returned to my temporary flat. These emotions were so intense that it had taken all my energy to ignore them while chatting to the friendly estate agent. I suddenly realized I could no longer ignore these thoughts or emotions if I did not want to feel broken anymore.

Initially, this acknowledgment seemed to make things more complex; I was acknowledging I had suicidal thoughts along with extreme emotions. Great! But where the hell was I go supposed to go from there? Over the course of the following two months, I went round and round in what felt like an endless washing machine cycle. I would get angry at my friend, then come back to a place of peace—you know, via a "peace and love" meditation or something—and then feel angry again soon after. What was I missing?

"Until you make the unconscious conscious, it will direct your life and you will call it fate"

—CARL JUNG—PSYCHIATRIST, PSYCHOANALYST & AUTHOR

That's when I happened to connect with Ela, the experienced life coach I had initially met online, whom I first mentioned in chapter nine. She offered me a complimentary coaching session that I gratefully accepted. She asked me if there was a specific situation she could help me with. I told her what happened, and her initial response was, "There were problems there before the outburst, weren't there?"

Holy crap.

The first of two realizations washed over me; for the first time, I openly acknowledged I had felt uncomfortable with a lot of things involving my soul-friend that I had ignored. Ela and I backtracked. Over multiple conversations where I had expressed my feelings, he had dismissed them. I had shared that I wasn't comfortable with some of his innuendos, but he dismissed this by telling me that I actually liked them. Confused about what our connection really was, I suggested some healthy boundaries, yet he became angry with me for suggesting this. Not wanting to lose his friendship, I backed down completely.

The point of all this was that I let him do this. No one was forcing me into this connection, and I continually put my feelings to the side as if they didn't matter, thinking I had no choice but to go along with what he said if I wanted his friendship. Ignoring parts of myself that were not happy had led to these extreme emotions and then thoughts of suicide. This suddenly seemed a very high price to pay for friendship.

This had been a pattern of behavior my whole life. I had repeatedly engaged in relationships with people who treated my feelings as if they were insignificant. I would convince myself I had no choice if I wanted them in my life, so I went along with whatever the other person wanted, even if it didn't feel good for me. I feared rejection so much that I rejected parts of myself instead.

I stayed in emotionally or physically abusive relationships in London in my late twenties, convincing myself I had no choice. It was as if I needed someone to blame for all these emotions instead of facing them. It also was not as if I was an innocent victim in these dynamics; there had been elements where I was manipulative as well. In this current dynamic with my friend, I had looked to him as someone who could "fix" me, so I kept desperately turning to him to do this. This was not a realistic or fair expectation, nor did it have the desired results.

All along, these emotions had been trying to get my attention; they were signposts toward a deeper understanding. For the first time in my life, I could visibly see how ignoring them had led to my own suffering. The pain that I thought was due to losing him as a friend was actually the pain of rejecting parts of myself. Tears rolled down my cheeks as I stared back at Ela, comprehending the enormity of what I had just acknowledged. For all these years, I believed it was the other person causing my suffering when, in actuality, I was causing my own suffering.

Now I felt stupid. How could I have done this? This is when the second realization hit me. There was an innocence in my behavior.

I had been completely unaware of this pattern until now. It did not excuse my unkind actions toward others over the years, but it went a long way to understanding the root cause. I could understand the real reasons behind my actions instead of making excuses or blaming them on other people or situations. Now I could actually finish the seemingly endless washing machine cycle. A sense of freedom had come from seeing things in a different way

The lesson I learned from this is that I do have a choice and that my emotions matter. Emotions are an extremely powerful personal guidance system, and ignoring them can result in extreme imbalances, including thoughts of suicide. This shifted my perspective on the subject of emotions because until now, I often felt as if putting my feelings first was selfish. Surely it was kind to take care of other people's feelings first? I now understood the consequence of this perception was that I rejected my own self. This created my own sense of brokenness.

Listening to ourselves is not being selfish. It is us recognizing our Wholeness.

This also marked a shift in how I regarded emotions themselves. Until this point, I had thought of them as something to be managed or controlled in some way, or even denied and ignored. A more helpful approach for me in daily life was to accept that emotions arise as a natural life phenomenon. I started to see how emotions are neither intrinsically good nor bad; they simply arise to make us more aware of what is happening in the present moment. It is being aware of their presence as a part of the experience of life. In getting caught up in the emotion, I had gone around in circles repeating unhelpful behavior. In acknowledging how I was feeling as well as moving into a space where I could reflect on what was really happening, it allowed for a deeper level of understanding. This was all that was needed to come back to a place of peace.

Instead of being scary, this session with Ela felt like one of the biggest reliefs in my life. All this time, this fear of my emotions had been a smokescreen. When I finally found the courage to walk through, it was surprisingly easy to do, although it still felt extremely uncomfortable in the actual moment.

A dear friend of mine, Karen, described these sensations beautifully to me one day. Her dad died of lung cancer when she was fourteen years old, yet the family simply continued with their lives, displaying little emotion. Karen followed suit, but this affected her life. She dropped out of several colleges and moved from one relationship to another, all while remaining in her job unhappily. In times when Karen has felt overwhelmed with emotions she describes it as feeling as though a volcano is about to erupt, yet when these emotions are allowed to be released, they overflow like the lava pouring out of a volcano. It is destructive, breaking down our current perception of things. Yet, it also leaves a new space with greater potential, much like the soil that settles after a volcano eruption is some of the most fertile in the world.

As the snow globe settled once more, from this point onward, I vowed to consider what my emotions were telling me, no matter how scary they felt in the moment or how much I might want to avoid them. Improving my relationship in this way with myself helped me to be more honest with others, which has opened up space for better-connected relationships. However, although I now saw situations along with my emotions in a more accepting way, I still had another deeper level of understanding I had to learn with my soul friend: what unconditional love really means.

Up to this point of the journey, I had been an avid learner, keen to understand myself ever more fully. However, there had been a sneaky undercurrent with all this inner learning. I was always looking for the next "thing" that might help me feel Whole; the next mentor, community, book, course, methodology, meditation, or something else. I liked to be continually adding "tools to my tool belt" so I could better equip myself to deal with daily life. Underneath all this, I was continually looking to the outside world for tools to "fix" the me that I still thought was broken. It did not matter that mentors or friends told me I was not broken. I did not believe them.

This constant seeking was exhausting. I had had enough of trying to develop myself. I started to question: "Is all this self-development work really as necessary as I believe, or is there a simpler solution?"

Sure enough, when the student is ready, the guide appears. This time what I learned was not through one exact experience but instead through developing a gradual understanding of the nature of thoughts themselves. When I look back at this time, I am shocked by how much simply changing my perception could bring a sense of ease into my life.

***

Reflection

Time and again since this session with Ela, the more I take time to contemplate what is going on underneath the surface level of emotions, the easier I find it to navigate life. I still feel all emotions with blazing intensity; however, taking a step back to identify the root causes behind emotions enables me to navigate *through* the storm instead of drowning within it. In turn, this has helped me to recognize there is always a level of peace underlying everything.

It does, however, require being *with* the emotions, not caught up in them. It is easy to see when we are ignoring emotions. From my own experience, some signs of ignoring emotions are:

- Pulling yourself together to work or be social
- Smiling when you want to cry or shout in anger
- Saying nothing when you feel hurt
- Hiding away from everyone because you feel too exhausted to pretend you are ok
- Giving others the "silent treatment" (not talking to them)
- Blaming or shaming others in some way
- Exploding into a rage and shouting at someone who has hurt you

If you can relate to any of these, or maybe you can think of other instances, then can you sit with the emotions to see what is going on underneath?

- Sit in a quiet place. What comes up? Notice all emotions, thoughts, and bodily sensations.
  - There is no thought that needs to be denied (such as "I want to kill them!") or "wrong" emotions that you "shouldn't be feeling."

    - Notice any body sensations—tightening or tension in certain areas. No need to change, fix or deny any of it.
    - You might want to write or record a voice note with what you notice. It is all information.
- If you can, stay until you notice a shift within you, signaling that you are ready to release. This can take five minutes or a lot longer.
    - You will know when you are ready because you will feel more at peace, like you are done.
- If you find it impossible to sit with your emotions because they are too intense, that's okay too. Instead, what fun activity can you do to shift yourself into a place of happiness?
    - It is from this space you are more likely to get insights into what is going on. Come back and sit down when you feel ready.
- Ask yourself, guides, the universe, or whatever/whoever you feel comfortable with, "What can I learn about myself?" or "What is going on underneath the surface that I need to see?"
    - Note that asking this when still caught up in the emotion does not often result in meaningful answers, so ask yourself this when you feel more at peace.
- There is a level of innocence in everything. Where might you unwittingly be causing your own suffering?
    - If you are not in a space where you can consider this, continue to sit with the emotions and thoughts. It takes as long as it takes!
- If you have found instances where you might be causing your own suffering or seen something beneath the surface, what needs to change to help you navigate better in the future?

There is no need for anything to change unless you are ready. Remember, this is not about other people changing. It is about how you can shift to better support yourself. Examples of types of changes are:

- Changing your tone with yourself or with others to be more supportive and caring.
- Asking deeper questions to yourself or others to identify the root causes behind behaviors or why things are not working properly.
    - Accept whatever answers come up. They are not right or wrong; they are simply an expression of what is happening.
- Take no action to see what happens next.
- Keep evaluating until you think of an action that seems appropriate. Action for the sake of action is often wasted effort.

When you feel ready, go back to your day and notice what differences there are in your outlook on life.

CHAPTER 11

What Was I Thinking?

Have you thought about the nature of your thoughts much? Until early 2021, I had not.

I kept *thinking*, as many of us do, that perhaps if I hire this coach, then I'll be happy. Perhaps if I read this self-help book, then I'll be happy. Perhaps if I learn about mindfulness or yoga or something, then I'll be happy. My underlying sense of brokenness was still present along with endless chattering of the mind, attempting to fix the "me" I still *thought* was broken.

As I became exhausted with continuously engaging in more self-development because I *thought* it would be good for me, this created space for a new understanding: looking at the nature of thoughts themselves.

In early 2021, I met and became friends with Helen, an experienced life coach. She shared with me a powerful story about her own life that helped me to understand more clearly the tendencies of my own mind.

Helen told me she was in the shower one morning, simultaneously running through her day in her head—thinking about who was picking up the kids, what time she was going to be home that night, along with other miscellaneous daily tasks. She thought, "*I'm going to be home at a decent time tonight. That means I'm a good mum.*" She noticed that she was suddenly feeling guilty. This was because she remembered that she was late the night prior and was thus, by her own stipulations, a bad mum. Then, a question arose: "Who decides what good parenting is anyway? Does it really make me a good mum just because I am home earlier tonight?"

Like a Jenga block being pulled out and collapsing the entire tower, the stories she believed around what factors must make a good mum started to collapse.

Helen described how her beliefs around the outward appearances of things she "should" do as a mum were subjective. Being home at a decent time didn't necessarily mean she was a good or bad mum; it was merely an interpretation her mind was making. Her mind was judging a particular situation, labeling activities as good or bad, then creating a story around who she was as a human being. All these years, she had innocently believed these mind-created stories to be the Truth, with a capital "T," as if they were absolutely True.

Every thought we have is a perspective—a subjective interpretation of what is happening at a particular point in time.

Our brain is wired to process, assume, and draw conclusions so that, by the time it reaches the conscious brain, we are given an extremely filtered, subjective view of the world.

Every brain will process the same information in a different way. This is widely known in cognitive behavioral science as our "Unconscious Bias." What we are each perceiving right now is a first-person subjective view of reality, not a third-person objective reality.

In the video "Do We See Reality as It Really Is?" Donald Hoffman, a cognitive scientist who has devoted his life to understanding consciousness, describes how our brain is designed to hide the complexities of reality to make it easier to live our daily life. He likens it to a folder icon on the computer; it provides an easy and efficient way to navigate the computer without having to know all the technical complexities behind it. So it is real, in the sense that you perceive a folder icon on your computer, and you know this is where to go if you wish to store and retrieve your online documents. It is also not true because the folder does not actually exist. Our brain acts in a similar fashion, creating a user interface to make it easier to navigate life.

Concepts like "normal" or "right" are probably the most common subjective interpretations; these naturally occur throughout daily life, hidden in plain sight. I started wondering, "*Who decides what is normal or right anyway*?"

As I worked with Helen over the coming months, I began to see many areas in my own life where I had an idea of a "right" or "normal" way to live life. I started to notice the endless conditional stories I had placed around my own happiness: "If I can work really hard to progress up the career ladder, if I can earn a bit more money, if I get more qualifications, if I can get my boyfriend to be my fairy tale prince, then I'll be happy." Most of these conditions were beyond my control; I cannot control my boyfriend, nor does a qualification guarantee a job, let alone happiness.

I was also deferring a sense of happiness to another point in time by insisting these conditions need to be met for happiness to exist in my life. It is as if my mind created a problem and then swooped in to "fix" it. No wonder I felt exhausted! I was constantly chasing happiness in the future when I can only live in the now.

I further began to notice all the times when I said "should" in my life. To me, using the word "should" is a red-light signal that I am referring to a predefined assumption of the way life is supposed to look. I noticed I used it a surprising amount throughout every single day. One of the most often "should" conditions I used was that I thought I *should* be happy because I have had many material opportunities available to me compared to the majority of the world— that's what people kept telling me anyway. I am, of course, extremely grateful to have them, but they also did not result in that inner feeling of happiness which then led to a feeling of guilt. I was finally beginning to resolve why I was so confused leaving London in chapter one.

External material opportunities did not mean my inner world was content. This continually resulted in conflict because my reality did not match up with other people's (or my own) subjective view of what reality *should* look like. I was, in effect, denying my reality as it presented itself. Whenever I was using the word "should," I noticed assumptions about how life needs to look, often from cultural influence from school, parents, family, or work. Sometimes I had no idea where they had even come from! Gradually, noticing all the times where I was "should-ing" over time, I began to distance myself from these assumptions as I could no longer buy into them anymore.

This began a shift for me away from many of the cultural assumptions I had grown up with. It has come with it a tinge of sadness, as with each time I see my "should-ing," I feel as though a small part of my assumed identity drops away. However, with this space comes an increasing sense of freedom, as I feel less and less bound by cultural or societal norms or even by my own interpretations or assumptions that I was previously unaware of. This increasing awareness is a lifelong endeavor.

I might not like what is happening, and I may still wish to change it; however, I can accept more easily that it is currently happening. This creates more space for bigger transformational shifts. It has started to take me truly on my own path as I began to see many global structures, processes, and systems we have in place in a different light.

I also began to understand there is no right or wrong about what the mind is doing. It is just what the mind does. For me, life moved from controlling or judging thoughts to accepting that they occur naturally throughout each moment of the day. Again, this created a different type of space. It has helped me move away from judgments about whether something is right or wrong. I began to see right and wrong as more subjective interpretations of the way the world needs to look. They are fine as concepts in contextualized situations; however, they became less absolute truths for me and more relative, subjective interpretations of what is occurring.

The danger of entering into an absolute idea of "wrong" is that this can lead to a rejection of life in some way. The universe naturally includes everything; it does not exclude anything. This is a type of Wholeness. The universe *is* and *does*. Spending time attempting to reject what already *is* suddenly seemed an extremely futile endeavor.

To me no two human beings have the exact same perception of life at the same moment, yet we are in the same singular universe. For me, it was now making less and less sense to spend time trying to convince anyone of anything. As I began to accept life more and more the way it is, again, I began to accept others the way they are as well. I then wondered if the global predominance of attempting to convince others of the "rightness" of a certain viewpoint could be the actual cause of frustrations, not the differences themselves.

In school, I remember participating in a debate at college about whether to remain part of the EU. The aim was to convince the judges that our team's point of view was more "right" than the other team. Our team won. Yes! We were "right," and I was proud of our victory. However, the consequence of believing there needs to be a right and wrong in this way meant half of the people there were labeled "wrong." They were excluded in some way. When this approach is repeated over and over as common behavior in our society, it impacts how we live together.

As I reflected on teachings such as this, I wondered if this is how we inadvertently create a separated, divided society. Perhaps this is a big source of conflict? What if, instead of debating to win, I had learned to discuss in a dialogue to live together peacefully as one humanity? You can see this conflicting approach everywhere, from the media to casual pub chat. Look at the language next time you listen to or read the news. Listen more deeply for implicit assumptions about how to live life, the judgments about right and wrong, and the insistence someone or something has to be to blame instead of seeking to understand and reconcile as one humanity.

It is my belief that peace in humanity can only exist by accepting each other's viewpoints as valid, no matter how much I might disagree with them. Perhaps it will be this acceptance that opens up the space for unity in humanity one day.

Additionally as part of this new understanding about the nature of thoughts I changed my perspective on the self-help tools I have at my disposal to support me in daily life, such as meditation, breathing techniques, yoga, or journaling. I still find them useful to me in certain moments; however, I no longer consider them necessary in the same regimented way my mind had been telling me.

In the past, I insisted on the importance of meditation every single day, whereas I now utilize it as a tool in moments only when I feel it will be beneficial. For some people, the support they feel they need might be meditating daily at the same time. However, for me, this does not work so well. In fact, upon reflection, it often created stress because it felt like a chore I thought I was supposed to do. Releasing myself from constraints such as this has brought much more ease into my life.

Over time, taking a step back to understand more deeply the nature of my thoughts has brought an enormous sense of freedom in so many aspects of my life.

I am here to be myself and not who someone thinks I should be. This has set me down a completely different life path, as my journey is no longer about fitting in with the world at all. I became more aware of the nature of my thoughts, which, when combined with everything else I had been learning, was moving me ever closer into a space to see what I am beyond all this. This continual observation of my thoughts allows me to let go of who I *thought* I was to make space for what I *truly* am.

So then the question becomes: "*Who am I, really?*"

***

Reflection

Understanding that my thoughts are a subjective interpretation of what is happening, like an inner dialogue or movie script, brought an enormous amount of relief. Consider the following:

- Who decides what is normal or right?
    - What is influencing this perspective?

- Next time you use the word "should," replace it with what is and is not happening. What changes?
  - What options open up to you?
  - What external influences are there behind your "should-ing"?
- Where in your life might you be labeling a person or group of people as "wrong" or "bad" that leads to their exclusion?
- If truth is a subjective and not absolute interpretation, what changes?

CHAPTER 12

Unconditional Love Is Freedom

"Who am I, really?"

I kept wondering about this, almost incessantly.

It was early 2021, five years after leaving my life behind in London. It was beginning to dawn on me that when I had departed, what I had really left behind was my self-created identity. During my time in London, I had projected an image of being invincible with the slogan "work-hard, play-hard," which I had now realized was driven by my fear of not being enough.

During my last year in London, I had been moving away from this image, but even then, a friend jokingly said to me one day, "You know, most of your stories start with 'This one time, when I was drunk……'" Drinking or partying was effectively my favorite hobby. I was working hard so I could enjoy this hobby of mine on evenings or weekends. As I reflected back on my first year of traveling after leaving London, I understood why I had felt so utterly rudderless. After I left my self-created identity back in London, I no longer had a career, nor did I drink much. I did not know who I really was without any of this.

This lack of identity, combined with persistent health issues, meant I continued searching for answers that did not come easily.

Shortly before returning home to the UK, I got an experiential glimpse of what I really am and what I believe we really are. By this time, I had moved from Hanoi to the coastal town of Da Nang in Vietnam. I was sitting in my living room on a typically hot and sticky day with the AC blasting out in my apartment to keep cool. I suddenly wondered what had happened to my Californian friend and hoped he was OK, as I had not heard from him, despite attempting to contact him.

As I wondered about this, I felt extremely sad that he was no longer in my life. With a sigh, I then thought, "*Ah well, there is nothing left to do but love him, whether we ever speak again or not.*" I wanted the door to be open to resuming our friendship at any time, still loving him unconditionally from afar if not. The crucial thing is that I meant this with all my heart.

Then, at that moment, something extraordinary happened while sitting in the apartment. A strong wave of energy started flowing up from the earth into the bottom of my spine, shooting up to flow out of the crown of my head and into the universe above, then down and round again. At the center point of my heart, it was as if a light suddenly shone out from it, radiating throughout my body and beyond.

My whole body tingled.

It felt similar to being high, except no drugs of any kind were involved, and the sensation was way beyond any I had ever taken. It was so strong I stopped what I was doing to lie down on the couch; I couldn't function properly at this point anyway. I "blissed" out.

I felt at peace, in harmony with myself and everything around me. I do not remember how long I stayed there, only that I wanted to lie in this feeling for as long as possible. Afterward, I thought, somewhat wryly, that if I had known I could get this high naturally, perhaps I would not have spent a decade of my life taking drugs. It is difficult to describe what it felt like to experience this life force pulsing through me; it was simply something beyond the chattering of the mind, the emotional guidance systems, or even my physical body.

I hope to remember this sensation forever because it was at this moment I went beyond an intellectual understanding of what unconditional love means; I *experienced* unconditional love. It was as if I was experiencing the "oneness" with myself and the universe.

Later, as the sensations subsided, I slowly picked myself up from the couch to go back to my day.

Everything felt different, more peaceful. It was an unanticipated moment of completely surrendering how I wanted life to look, namely that I was in contact with my friend, and instead fully accepting the situation as it was in that present moment, including the sadness I felt about it. This seemed to open a gateway to experiencing a connection to our Wholeness.

It was at this point I understood our fundamental "okay-ness," peace or oneness that is already available, including when experiencing sadness or pain of some sort. I now understood that we could, paradoxically, be both happy and sad at the same time. Life can include everything simultaneously. This is what true unity or oneness means to me. This opened so many opportunities—if holding paradoxes was possible, then anything was possible. Since this experience, I have increasingly felt this unconditional love as a consistent undercurrent in my life.

Over the coming months after this experience, I reflected further on my past relationships with friends or boyfriends. I realized that often I did nice things, such as buy a gift or pay for a meal, but I often expected this kindness to be returned to me in some way. I had been putting conditions around extending love to people everywhere. This meant I had been trapping myself because I often got upset when I did not feel that my kindness had been reciprocated sufficiently. In experiencing this, I could see the freedom that comes from unconditionally loving someone; it removes expectations that trap me.

Once again, I had unwittingly been causing my own suffering.

I had the pleasure of connecting with Azim Khamaiza, who tragically lost his son when he was murdered delivering pizza in 1995. His response was perhaps not what most of us would expect. Following what Azim described as an "out-of-body experience" when he learned of his son's death, he came back immediately with an understanding that has shaped the rest of his life:

"There are victims on both ends of the gun."

For Azim, it was not intellect or even emotions that supported him at this time. It was his already strong sense of unconditional love for all of humanity, no matter what happens. This had been cultivated throughout his life from a young age. It also enabled him to see there are other perspectives. Namely that of his son's killer, Tony, who had grown up in a violent gang culture; he simply did not know anything other than violence at that point.

I was surprised to learn that five years later, Azim went to visit Tony in prison. Although it was difficult, Azim said he saw the same spark of humanity in Tony as in everyone else. This was possible by seeing every human through a lens of unconditional love. In turn, this gave Tony the motivation he needed to turn his life around. He studied in prison, then when he was released twenty-five years later, they started to work alongside each other to raise awareness of the danger of gang violence. Together they provide a beautiful example that there is always unconditional love available underneath, no matter how grave a situation appears to be.

Unconditional love extends to the whole of humanity. In this way, it is the thing that connects us all as one Whole being.

Following this experience, more of my beliefs started to crumble. For most of my life, I had been acting as if there were battles to be fought. Not the traditional wars we see around the world, but battles within myself. There were battles to control my thoughts, battles to settle my digestive system, and battles to control my emotions to keep from falling apart.

It manifested itself in the way I viewed the world; I acted as if there were battles to be fought against people who did not agree with me to get them to see things from my point of view. However, I found I could no longer understand fighting anything.

In loving everything exactly as it is right now, there is nothing to fight against; love does not understand anything other than peace. Even if I am fighting what I have decided is a "good fight," I am still fighting a fight. I knew the next phase of my life was to explore this sense of unity further over the coming years and what impact it can have on our one Whole humanity.

My entire perception of life has been gradually shifting toward answering a question that I will probably never fully be able to answer in this lifetime because the question can take me in so many different directions: *What does it take to allow each of us to personalize our life while embodying Wholeness as One United Humanity?*

***

Reflection

This type of sensation is something that has to be experienced, not explained. There is no "how to love?". It either happens, or it does not. If you do not feel this, as I did not for most of my life, then there is something blocking this. Take a look:

- Where in your life are you placing conditions around loving and being loved?
  - What are those conditions?
- Where have these conditions come from?

While this story relates to loving someone else unconditionally, it is equally important to love yourself unconditionally. Consider:

- Where in your life are you not behaving in an unconditionally loving way toward yourself?
  - What is preventing this?
  - What could you do to change this?

PART 5

CONTINUING: FROM INDIVIDUAL TO WHOLENESS

CHAPTER 13

Wholeness in Humanity

I believe treating ourselves as a Whole Human has the potential to impact the entire human race. Listening to all parts of ourselves, in turn, changes the way we listen to and connect with others. Our relationship with ourselves reflects our relationships with each other.

My friend Ayu experienced a momentous shift in her own circumstances by changing her relationship with herself, not only in her own life but also in the lives of those around her. She suffered from chronic illness for much of her life and had also been in an abusive marriage that caused her to lose access to see her daughter when she left. As she learned to listen deeply to all parts of herself, her health was restored. This, in turn, opened the gateway to restoring a healthy connection with her ex-husband and therefore regaining access to her daughter as well.

Her experience was so inspirational to me that I have shared it in Case Study One. I hope that it inspires those who may be struggling with ill health, blame, or hurt in some way, as well as illustrating the positive impact a Whole Human approach can have on all aspects of our lives.

Consider this question, though: If we all approached our lives as Whole Humans, what would society look like?

Ayu's experience is from a personal perspective. However, the same Whole Human approach can impact anything. Let's take businesses as an example. After all, businesses are made up of human beings; more specifically, how the people in a business can function in a Whole Human way by uncovering what is not working (part one) and then understanding where the disconnections are (part two). It requires an understanding that we are all interconnected (part three). When coming from these understandings, it becomes possible to move into newly discovered spaces that allow us to identify and resolve the root causes of issues (part four). What really makes everything work is when coming from a place of unconditional love. I believe the reflections at the end of the chapters can apply equally in a business or any other setting.

I began to connect with people experimenting with conducting business from a Whole Human perspective. In the following sections, I have summarized a few of these examples that inspire me greatly. I hope they inspire you too.

Whole Human Healthcare: Buurtzorg

When I had hip surgery at thirty years old, I felt like a ping-pong ball going back and forth between departments in the UK's National Health Service (NHS) as I attempted to get scans done. It appeared that departments did not communicate with each other nor have processes that worked. I went to my doctor several times, phoned different departments, then personally visited different hospitals in an effort to get the scans. I suddenly managed to get an appointment coincidentally when their own targets for seeing patients were about to be missed. I felt like a number, not a human. Yet, at the same time, I remember feeling that all those humans—the doctors and nurses—genuinely wanted the best outcome for me as the patient.

We were all enmeshed in the complicated bureaucracy. Eventually, I opted to have hip surgery outside of the NHS because, despite the well-meaning professionals, I did not trust the system. I was fortunate that this was an option for me; for many, this is not possible. It appeared the system was not geared toward supporting the human—neither the patients nor doctors and nurses. Instead, it was centered around the systems. Having lived, studied, and experienced the most completely holistic medicine I have found to date, Ayurveda, I was also wondering whether some of its general holistic principles can be applied to modern healthcare systems.

I chatted with Jos de Blok, the CEO and founder of Buurtzorg, a company established in the Netherlands. When I first heard about them, I was excited to learn about their approach to healthcare because the way they treat their patients is aligned with seeing them as Whole Humans. Jos himself started out as a community nurse some years ago. At the time, he had a lot of autonomy to work with other professionals directly, utilize informal networks available within the community, as well as respond to the needs of the patient as they occurred.

He could work in a focused, connected network on a daily basis, centered around the patient.

However, over time, more management layers were combined with the fragmentation of the system, notably splitting health and social care, along with a shift to focus on profits instead of patients. He found it increasingly difficult to provide the care he felt the patients needed. So Buurtzorg was born to return to patient-centered, personalized, holistic healthcare that is interconnected with the community.

Their approach is proving successful; the organization has grown to 15,000 nurses across twenty-five countries. As the company expanded, he found the problems experienced to be similar worldwide. "We started working with different countries and discovered that the problems are the same. The message every time is to start again from the patient perspective and simplify the systems."

Jos described to me the simple Buurtzorg model. Front line staff collaborates together to support the patient directly in their home environment. The staff builds their own informal networks within the community that includes health and social care together so they can support what the patients want. They do not have any real management hierarchies. They have a simple financial model with single pricing using minimal technology that is sufficient enough to get the job done.

At the same time, the frontline nurses are relieved of a lot of the administration work, which is done centrally instead, so they can spend the majority of their time with the patients.

Yet their administration team is extremely small, with only fifty employees for all 15,000 nurses. Jos told me that wherever they operate, they simultaneously improve the quality of care, reduce the number of hours of care needed, and improve employee and patient satisfaction. Patients treated under the Buurtzorg model end up needing fewer visits to hospitals as well as spending less time in hospital than patients who are treated with the predominant western model of healthcare.

From examples such as this, I have started to seriously question whether the complicated processes and systems requiring huge IT infrastructure as well as a lot of staff to manage it, no matter what industry they are in, are as inevitable or unavoidable as is often thought. Perhaps all it takes is a few people willing to experiment in a different way.

Although my experience relating to my hip is a little different from this outpatient care, I believe the simplified principles that center around the patient while allowing professionals to do their job effectively can still apply. I also wonder if this type of care centered around the patient, directly within their environment, could help to reverse the increasing trend of chronic illnesses I mentioned in the Introduction. As I witnessed at MTC in chapter four, treating patients as one Whole Human can have a tremendous impact on their lives.

It can also apply to other industries; do companies really center around the needs of the Whole Human, or do they seek to convince us our lives would be better with certain items, more specifically what they are selling? Following my experience in chapter ten, where I suddenly saw the difference between convincing or "selling" something instead of collaborating together, I now question the entire idea that anyone needs to be sold anything. If you start from the perspective of the Whole Human and keep things as simple as possible, how could this impact any company in any industry?

Buurtzorg is an example of an organization doing things from a Whole Human perspective from the outset. However, I am also keenly interested in exploring whether or not the tremendous cultural change to focus on the Whole Human can happen organically from the people within an existing organization.

Holistic Cultural Change: Alzheimer's Society and Zoom Creates Ltd.

A good friend of mine, Barry Holmes, is a keen advocate of my favorite topic: Wholeness in daily life. We have had many conversations surrounding this. He has explored Wholeness through continuously experimenting with different styles of learning in corporate environments over the last twenty years. At the beginning of the pandemic in 2019, his company, Zoom Creates Ltd, which is operated as a team with his brother Mark Holmes, partnered with the Alzheimer's Society to support them with their desire to genuinely empower their staff as well as shift the traditional Command-And-Control style culture.

Becky, head of Learning & Organizational Development, told me that the management team was fed up with traditional leadership training that focused on abstract theories or how to take minutes and write reports. They wanted something entirely different. What Alzheimer's Society and Zoom Creates Ltd are exploring together is a totally different style of learning, a course called "Perspectives" that embeds a change in culture naturally.

It is gradually shifting the entire organization from a traditional Command-and-Control style structure toward a genuinely participatory style of working. It is being supported by employees participating in learning that removes hierarchical separation and centers around listening to each other and ingraining an appreciation that different perspectives are a normal part of life instead of a direct challenge to their position within the company. The idea is that learning is focused on impacting the Whole Human on a personal level, which improves their ability to perform their role at the worker level.

I share details on how they are doing this and the impact so far in Case Study Two: Everything Interconnects. I believe this is a potential way that existing models can be shifted; however, it does take time and a sustained effort. It is also a possible route to make gentle corrections for overshoots, which Donella Meadows and Jorgan Randers speak about in their book *Limits to Growth* (2004) (which was mentioned previously in the introduction of this book). This is an example that has caused me to question how to change when existing models are not working:

- Is it always that new models need to be built when existing ones are not working, or can existing models shift?
- What does it take to shift?

- Where are we shifting toward?

Whole Human Learning

As I looked back at the depths I had explored into myself as well as what I hope to continue exploring in the future, I reflected on whether society is set up to support and encourage this type of exploration, or in other words, learning. Since this type of learning brings me so much happiness, it is one of my biggest hopes that it can be available for anyone who wants to engage in this, no matter where or who they are.

So many aspects of myself explored in this book were not included in the education I received growing up. As an example, one of my teachers told me that one-third of my year had either eating or mental health disorders. Yet, nothing was spoken about this openly, nor was it addressed within the school learning environment. The more I considered my education, the more it became apparent how little input I had into it; the curriculum was almost totally predefined. I could choose A-levels, but these were still all academic options. The focus of learning was geared toward passing the exam, not exploring my own passion for subjects in a holistic way. Very little of the education system I went through was set up to support this style of learning.

I was chatting with Thom Markham, who has played a lead role in developing Project Based Learning (PBL) in schools over the last twenty-five years. PBL is based on engaging students in meaningful projects where they can develop their whole selves while still covering the content of the curriculum. It is one example of the way in which learning can be altered to support more of our whole selves. Children still learn the content needed to pass exams, but through a project-based approach, they learn interpersonal skills by working with others as well as engage in self-reflection throughout the project. Real-life problems are identified, making knowledge applicable instead of abstract theory.

Thom has worked with over two hundred schools to mentor their teachers to transition to this type of learning. He believes the time of a teacher standing in front of a classroom telling a student what to learn is being seriously challenged now. In the future, students will have more "voice and choice" to guide their own learning with support from the educator, who takes on more of a mentor-style approach instead.

Although the aim of PBL is not simply to pass exams, there is evidence that this approach to learning outperforms traditional-style learning (Saavedra 2021). Additionally, this better performance includes students of color and those from low-income backgrounds; it can benefit everyone.

I know that my teachers had my best intentions at heart; they were especially supportive when I was ill with glandular fever at sixteen years old. Some of my teachers even sat with me one-on-one to ensure I caught up with work. It also helped me to into a career that gave me the financial backing to support me through this different type of exploration into who I really am. However, although I got grades in school, I did not enjoy the experience. What is the point if I am not enjoying it?

It is not that this type of education is necessarily wrong; this type of academic education may absolutely suit some people, but given that we are all unique, we all learn differently and have very different passions. So is it realistic that one type of education is capable of supporting every Whole Human?

The last six years of my life had been experiential learning through listening, observing, and reflecting as an integrated part of actually living daily life. So much of what I learned did not need a classroom. I learned what I needed as each new challenge arose, as I believe we all do throughout life. Most of my learning was experiential, not academic. The numerous people that supported me throughout this process were more like guides or mentors, encouraging me to learn for myself rather than teaching me anything. I now firmly believe that education is not something that needs to be done in a classroom, nor is it only for children. It is a lifelong endeavor and what is available for us to learn is as infinite as the universe itself. We also learn *from* and *with* each other. Consider these questions:

- If you had the opportunity to learn absolutely anything you wanted, what would it be?
- What and where would be the ideal environment to learn be?
- If anyone could learn anything, anytime from anywhere, what would the world look like?

An approach such as this seems more connected with what businesses themselves are beginning to want. Even companies hiring for white-collar jobs are shifting from a preference for university-educated people to people who can connect with others. They need employees with interpersonal skills to run a business successfully.

According to a *Business Insider* article by Allana Akhtar, published in December 2020, big companies such as Tesla, Apple, Google, and Netflix are becoming less fixated on a degree, questioning whether a university degree adequately prepares workers. I looked at the Google employment page titled "How We Hire." Their first step is not how to apply or what they are looking for; it is that the candidate is firstly engaging in their own self-reflection. In other words, even Google is interested in people who are exploring themselves first.

Approaching life from a perspective of Wholeness has its challenges. Jos noted that when he speaks to governments about the Buurtzorg approach to providing healthcare, a big challenge is what to do with the large number of people that manage activities that would no longer be needed if their model was adopted. Barry told me that not everyone likes or understands their "Perspectives" training, as they offer no answers and only aim to provide better questions to seriously challenge the existing ways of doing things; some people still want to be told what to do.

Thom indicated parents themselves are often divided when it comes to the discussion of education; some want their children to be educated in a traditional way while others want a different style to be available. This is a powerful reminder to me that the next phase of my life is not about convincing anyone of anything; we each learn or change in a way that makes sense to us personally.

***

The next steps for me involve connecting more and more with those who wish to embody Wholeness with Wholeheartedness, even if we currently do know exactly how that might happen. To me, life is really lived from questions, not definite answers. It has become my lifelong endeavor to explore this question:

What does it take to be able to live in a society that embodies Wholeness?

CHAPTER 14

Case Study One

Listening To Each Other

There is perhaps no one else in my life who better understands the interconnections of listening than my friend Ayu, whom I first met in Bali. Learning about her journey inspired me because she beautifully illustrates the connections between our relationships with ourselves and others. This, in turn, can shift entire, seemingly impossible conflicts toward a unified and peaceful approach to living with each other.

Ayu grew up in a traditional Balinese village in Indonesia, in a family where violence was normal. Her father was abusive toward her mother as well as Ayu herself and other members of the household. Ayu constantly felt unsafe, as well as ashamed of the abuse and lying. Ayu believed everyone must simply be bad, including herself. Over time this impacted her health. Ayu was frequently ill, sometimes suffering from inexplicable paralysis of the legs or intense fevers. In addition to this, suicidal, judgmental thoughts would run around her head, and despite going to doctors and shamans, which are commonly consulted in Indonesia, no cause or resolution could be found.

As was expected in her village, she married and gave birth to a daughter. Her marriage was abusive, yet her family told her to accept this and stay quiet. As she had her daughter to think about, she left her husband. In Balinese culture, automatic rights are not given to the mother, so her daughter went to live with the father. Her father could not take care of her, but rather than letting Ayu take care of their daughter, the child went to the father's grandmother instead. Ayu was angry at this seemingly incomprehensible decision, blamed him, and concluded that he was a malicious human being. Her health continued to decline as she suffered from bouts of temporary paralysis or fevers.

Years later, after one episode of illness that lasted for almost six weeks, along with the all-too-familiar suicidal thoughts, Ayu was totally exhausted. She had been blaming her current ill health on her upbringing and her abusive ex-husband, but now she was even exhausted with this. One morning she woke up with the realization it was not that she wanted to die; it was that she did not know what to do; this was the real source of her frustration. In that moment, a voice told her to listen to the pain instead of getting frustrated. Out of other options, she had nothing left to lose but to try this approach.

As she identified pain in her body, she listened to whatever thoughts or emotions came up, trusting that the physical pain was linked to this even if she could not understand the link logically or scientifically. She sat listening intently, as she would for a good friend, without judging, denying, or even attempting to fix anything. No thought was a bad thought or to be dismissed, and no emotion was too scary or avoided. She continued listening for four days straight. No matter what the pain, how outrageous the thought, or how intense the emotion felt, she listened without judgment or attempting to change anything. She simply listened.

After this, she started to feel more grounded, more human, more Whole. Over the following months, whenever she was in pain, she would stop to listen to whatever was arising. She found the more she did this, the more her health began to recover, and she had steadily increasing energy. She no longer suffered from paralysis or fever.

In learning to listen to herself, Ayu also changed how she listened to others. As she realized she was not the bad or shameful human she had believed previously, she began to think perhaps others were not either, including her ex-husband. In any case, she was as exhausted with judgments and blaming of others as she was with judging or blaming herself, so she was again prepared to try a different approach. She wanted to see if there was something beyond the surface-level "bad" actions of her ex-husband.

As Ayu felt physically safe sitting down with her ex-husband, she decided to arrange to meet him with one purpose only: to listen to him. She made this intention clear to him at the beginning. She was not there to judge or even fix anything. At first, he was taken aback. However, he was open to talking, and Ayu learned a different side to the story. He admitted he felt an immense amount of shame as he was unable to take care of his own daughter and had to give her to his mother.

It turned out he had a great fear that Ayu would take her daughter from him, which led him to make it difficult for Ayu to keep in contact with her daughter.

Listening to him, Ayu realized how hard it had been for him as well. They talked for four hours, and he shared that he had been trapped in a culture of intergenerational violence as much as she had. At the end of this lengthy chat, they agreed to resume communications so they could figure out together how their daughter could have both parents in her life without conflict. Today, they have a friendly relationship, figuring out the parenting together. It has not always been easy for either of them; however, it has brought a further sense of peace for Ayu, her husband, their daughter, and their families.

Since the cycle of abuse that was passed down multiple generations has now ended, Ayu's daughter can grow up in a peaceful environment instead.

Ayu now works with others who want to learn to communicate with others in a compassionate way. She takes them on a journey similar to her own; her clients learn to listen to themselves first, then learn techniques to interact in a caring way with others afterward. Ayu had no way of knowing what the outcome would be when she listened to herself or to her ex-husband. All she could do was create the environment to open up an opportunity for a more loving, more connected way to live. Fortunately for Ayu, her ex-husband was willing to connect, talk and listen, much in a way Ayu had for herself first.

This may not always be the case for everyone, but it shows the enormous potential to shift from conflict to peace simply by listening to each other, and putting all judgment, blame, or assumptions aside.

Are you ready to listen deeply?

CHAPTER 15

Case Study Two

Everything Interconnects

"It is about wholeness and integration at work rather than separation."

—*BARRY HOLMES, CO-FOUNDER OF ZOOM CREATES LTD*

"I was a cardboard cutout at work," remarked Kelly, one of the area managers I spoke with at Alzheimer's Society.

Kelly is passionate about her job yet knew she was not always as effective as she could be in the workplace. No one really understood why she was in the organization other than the shared aim of wanting to support people with dementia. She did not bring her Whole Self to work nor share what really drives her. At the beginning of the COVID-19 pandemic, Kelly was one of the first participants in a novel type of training from Zoom Creates Ltd called "Perspectives." Although Kelly enjoys any learning that supports her personal growth, she was also a little doubtful. Was this yet another boring management training, teaching her abstract theorems or how to take minutes and write reports?

Many of us have been in this situation at some point, sitting in a classroom, being told what to do or how to think to attain the (purported) best results.

Alzheimer's Society is a health and social care organization that previously functioned largely via a Command-and-Control style of management that is prevalent in many sectors today. The term "Command-and-Control" was initially a military term defined as "The facilities, equipment, communications, procedures, and personnel essential for a commander to plan, direct, and control operations of assigned and attached forces pursuant to the missions assigned" (Department of Defense Dictionary of Military and Associated Terms 2016). This style of structure may be suited to military matters or even for manufacturing; however, it is less suitable when considering sectors that focus on people requiring personalized care directly in their environment. This type of care lends itself to people who can think on their feet, take the initiative, and solve problems using the resources around them.

The leadership team recognized the need to change, although they did not know how. Fully supported by the CEO, managers wanted a learning style that modeled the reality they work in while also encouraging them into uncomfortable spaces, enabling them to grow simultaneously as individuals as well as managers within their organization. The Learning & Organizational Development at Alzheimer's Society was tasked with addressing this. They partnered with a learning company, Zoom Creates Ltd, that demonstrated a deep understanding of this need and offered an alternative approach. The learning model "Perspectives" is the creation of two brothers, Barry and Mark Holmes. They have facilitated learning for many of the world's biggest companies, such as Visa, L'Oréal, Deloitte, and DHL, for over two decades.

They believe that to shift a culture requires a shift on a personal level, not the worker level. There is no "how-to" in the course. It is not about acquiring more knowledge, adopting best practices, or copying other models that have succeeded; instead, they focus around creating the space for change to happen naturally. This is done through exploration in a group. Crucially the group is a mix of different levels and areas of the organization. This means that right from the beginning, the Command-and-Control style management layers present in the organization did not matter in this space. Everyone is equal and exploring together as one.

Over the duration of the thirteen-week course, they speak with people in many different areas of the organization. They are exposed to so many different perspectives during this time that it becomes normal to expect diverse viewpoints on the same topic. Instead of feeling challenged by this, it becomes a natural part of discussions.

Right from the first session, Kelly learned some simple yet critical points that went on to have a huge impact on her job. Firstly, she learned the importance of listening to hear the other person, not simply responding immediately with her opinion. She noticed that as she took a step back, other quieter members of the group contributed more, which in turn enhanced the richness of their discussions. It only took a few sessions before Kelly felt this space had become a place where she herself could suggest and explore different ideas about how the organization could look without needing to consider, in Kelly's words, "whether it was professional suicide to speak out."

In their sessions, they modeled the real environment, namely the workplace, but within a space that was safe because it was simply exploration time where everyone journeys together. Through conversation over the weeks, patterns of issues were found naturally, which were then explored, leading to improvements in the way the company works. She realized the enormous opportunities that open up through this type of guided conversation as well as how fun it can be.

In between each week, reflection time is strongly encouraged. Kelly herself built an hour and a half into her schedule. She found this so beneficial that she maintained it long after the training was completed. To her, it is a critical time to evaluate what is or is not working well or what she could learn from other people. In her operations role, it can be more reactive than she would like, so this gives her an opportunity to shift to become more proactive instead. Zoom Creates also continue to offer guidance once the official course has finished, giving time for employees to integrate what has been learned into their daily roles. They do this by providing a space every week to discuss any work problem someone in the group wants to share. This ongoing support helps to embed as well as continue cultural shifts in the company.

After the course, Kelly changed the way she worked significantly. She now has specific time out with her team to focus on strategy—where they would like to be versus where they are today. She feels that everyone knows why she is here and what they can contact her for within the organization. She notices that her team now proactively contacts her, whereas previously, she often had to chase them. This in itself makes her role a lot easier. In turn, this frees up time and mental capacity for other things that can add genuine value to the organization.

She also realized the importance of supporting the Whole person, especially during the pandemic. One of her staff was troubled because she was living in the UK, whereas her parents were in Portugal but struggling to take care of themselves. Since everyone was working from home by this point anyway, Kelly decided she could work from Portugal, a decision Kelly said she would not have had the courage to make prior to the training.

Kelly has noticed the culture seems to be shifting from the executive giving orders in a typical Command-and-Control style structure to listening and then responding to what their staff on the front line are saying. To Kelly, her own team's response to the annual engagement survey speaks volumes. Whereas previously, she had to chase her team repeatedly to reply, in their most recent survey, every team member completed it by the end of day two. They are engaging because they know what they say matters and that management is listening.

At the same time, it is impacting how they interact with their clients, the very reason they exist in the first place. The frontline staff feels more able to take the initiative to respond in a holistic, non-prescriptive way. Previously there had been a lot of processes to handle clients in a standard way, whereas each client can have very bespoke needs. Kelly recalled one of their patients had become isolated within his house because he had fallen out with his neighbors. He was physically unable to walk to the bins that were located far from his house, so the rubbish built up in his garden, which looked a state as well as encouraging vermin, much to the annoyance of his neighbors.

They did not know he had dementia, and he was unable to communicate this properly with them.

So the patient stayed in his house to avoid his neighbors, which led to him feeling very low. The frontline staff, now feeling empowered to take the initiative, decided to speak with the refuse collectors to explain the situation, who then began to collect the rubbish from outside his house instead. The care worker then arranged a meeting with the neighbors with the patient present to explain the situation. A cleanup was organized for the garden that the council agreed to pay for. Now he has a lovely relationship with his neighbors as well as the refuse collector, even exchanging presents at Christmas.

The benefits of greater autonomy on a personal level are that it tends to positively impact our health. In a 2021 study by Erik Gonzalez-Mulé and Bethany S. Cockburn titled "This job is (literally) killing me: A moderated-mediated model linking work characteristics to mortality," they found that workers who have greater control over their workflow also tend to be more healthy and have less negative health impacts than those in similar work positions that have less flexibility or control.

With this new perspective on bringing your Whole Self to work, Kelly began to reflect on whether she brings her Whole Self into relationships. She reflected that she had been presenting the cardboard cutout version of herself in her recently ended relationship. While there are always many dimensions to the ending of a relationship, now she could see that this could have affected it.

She began to shift with her children as well, considering what they might need beyond cooking for them or paying for items—in other words, seeing them as Whole Humans too. The cardboard cutout that Kelly thought she was supposed to be at work has gone. She is much more herself, not only at work but also in other areas of her life. Kelly remarked that being this cardboard cut-out had been extremely hard work. Though, she has found that being herself in all areas of life now requires a lot less energy. Kelly illustrates the interconnections between aspects of our lives; an impact in one area can impact another. We are not separate selves in different areas of our lives. For Kelly, the "Perspectives" course was definitely not a standard form of management training.

However, everyone has their own experience during the training, and not everyone has understood or liked it. Barry told me that their "Perspectives" learning program is specifically designed to question everything around leadership, bring in alternative views, and slow down and open up space for contemplation—something that is not always appreciated.

However the course has been deemed successful so Alzheimer's Society continues to offer it to all leaders and managers within the organization, which is a testament to how important they believe this type of learning is to continue their cultural shift as well as simultaneously caring for their staff, all while improving front line services. Becky, the head of Learning & Organizational Development at Alzheimer's Society, has indicated that more time is needed to really embed the learning. Changing culture is not a quick fix and requires commitment from all involved.

I believe this type of approach to learning has huge possible implications because improving work effectiveness does not necessarily mean spending on expensive new IT systems, creating new processes to patch over failing ones, or increasing control mechanisms. Barry has found that, at times, it has been possible to change the perception of job satisfaction itself without even changing the role of the employee. This all started from an understanding of the interconnectedness of life, not an understanding of how organizations should be structured.

Perhaps the solutions to many of the challenges with our current complex systems and processes are similar to the challenges around being our Whole Selves throughout life; maybe all it requires is to start having connected conversations.

CHAPTER 16

The Journey Continues

On some level, I always knew I could not settle anywhere until I had settled in myself.

I almost bought a beautiful two-bed flat in London two years before leaving on my journey but backed out because something did not feel right. Eight years after pulling out of buying that flat, I finally felt ready to settle. I knew my stay in Vietnam was coming to a close, and it was time to return home. I booked my ticket, sold what few possessions I had acquired in Vietnam, then made my way back to Hanoi, the capital.

I was sad to leave, yet I knew I was ready for something else. Even if I did not know what that was.

As I sat looking out of the plane window, I reflected back to when I first got on a plane to travel. Back then, I had no idea where I was going. I mean, I knew from a geographical standpoint, but I had no idea the depth of the journey I would go into myself nor how far my approach to life would change. I did not leave London because I had any clarity or answers. On the contrary, I left because I did not know at all. Yet, my entire journey of traveling and living abroad has not brought the knowledge I initially hoped it would. Instead, life became easier because I became okay with not knowing.

If you are hesitating about making some change in your life right now but do not know what to do, then not knowing is all the information needed. The next steps always became apparent for me, and it is my belief they will become so for you, too. You do not always need to know the destination; you only need to watch for the next step to become obvious. The next step is always somewhere nearby if you are vigilantly looking for it.

Where is your next step?

The brokenness I felt when I began my journey was because I could not see the deeper levels of disconnection. Being seen as a Whole Human by Doctor Sundara impacted me far beyond what I initially imagined. It was like a snowball effect that led me down paths to question my life ever more deeply. As my body, mind, and even my soul screamed at me for attention that could not be ignored, I began discovering enormous opportunities to shift the direction of my life. As I went along my journey, I gradually understood the real source of my unhappiness and ill health was because of the disconnected way I had been living.

Time and time again, I found the real disconnections when looking beyond the surface level of what appears to be happening to see the root cause of what is actually happening. As I established better connections with my Whole Self, this also brought in a sense of ease with life as well as trusting in the natural flow of life. The way to settle myself had been by cutting through what did not make sense or what was causing me pain. There was no way around it nor any shortcut. Every time I went down a new path into a new space, no matter how uncomfortable it was at first, it opened opportunities to see things in a different way. Sometimes that in itself was all that was needed to restore a sense of balance. As my perspective on life shifted toward a belief that we are one interconnected universe, this contributed to an underlying sense of peace within myself.

Crucially, by asking deeper, more expansive questions, as well as being willing to entertain new ideas, ways of doing, thinking, or being led to better health and happiness, I hope I have inspired a deeper questioning of life. If you are unhappy or feel as though you are struggling, maybe it is a signal that there is more available in life than you thought up until now. It is up to each of us to own our investigations. No one can do this for us.

Where could you be unwittingly disconnected? What could be happening beyond the surface level of what you initially see?

My feelings of anxiety reduced drastically as I came to view life in a more Whole, complete way. I worried less and less about whether I was making the "right" decision when moving. Instead, I started to view my decisions as the path I had chosen that would lead to learning. Without anything to deny, this has made life a lot easier. Nothing else has actually changed in this respect—only my approach.

Having spent years struggling with IBS, I still feel joy in each day my bowel movements work in a regular, healthy manner; it is a daily reminder of how much I have changed along my journey so far. The unbearable pain from my menstrual cycles gave me the opportunity to understand the difference between masculine and feminine energies as well as the necessity of the balance between them. Appreciating this balance guides me differently.

The heartbreak that forced me to pause everything meant I learned the difference between taking action because I believed it was what I was supposed to do and taking action that genuinely supports my Whole being. The pain of losing my soul friend led to a deeper connection with my emotions, which meant I could finally identify the root cause of unhelpful patterns of behavior. It also led me to experience unconditional love.

After the treatments at MTC, I have yet to have an infection requiring medication. Since moving to Brighton on the south coast of England in December 2021, I have yet to have a migraine. The more of my Whole Self I acknowledge, the better my overall health becomes. My menstrual cycles keep improving, although I still experience pain, which signals to me that there is a deeper level of understanding I have yet to see, and I will keep questioning until I figure this out.

When the plane touched down, I was extremely grateful for my adventures so far. It had been a brilliant ride to be absorbed in different cultures, all intermingled with experiencing different aspects of myself. However, the thing I had learned about moving every few months was that, as exciting as it was to be able to do this, over time, I began to miss the depth of connections that are made with people that happen over time.

Our approach to change is a very personal thing. Change is something that happens all the time throughout the universe; the only constant in the universe is change itself. Most of us have no idea what thoughts will pop into our minds in the next ten minutes, let alone throughout a lifetime. Unexpected twists happen regularly, whether they are happy or disastrous turns. Uncertainty is woven into our very existence. Stability in life is therefore not about creating certainty.

To me, stability is creating the conditions where, when the snow globe is next shaken, I have the ability to adjust to the new landscape that settles around and within me. Living is about how I choose to handle these situations as they unexpectedly arise rather than whether I choose to experience them. Throughout life, there are continuous opportunities to explore the nature of Wholeness through leaving and coming back to it. The ability to adjust comes from an inner knowledge about ourselves as well as a connection to natural life cycles.

My journey is not over. It has only just begun. I know now that I can accept current situations while simultaneously working to open up realistic opportunities for humanity to live as one connected being.

By the time I returned home, I was seriously questioning how all these angles of connection I explored in myself, as well as the interconnected flow of life, could apply to society as well.

My approach to life has changed completely because now I believe life is about how we choose to connect, not whether we choose to connect. It has led me to ask an intriguingly exploratory question about humanity itself: How do we want to connect with each other in modern, daily life?

As I settled into Brighton in 2022, I woke up one sunny but cold spring morning to notice I have a desire to live life. From all this exploration, I finally shifted from feeling broken to Whole. A huge part of the excitement in my next adventure is exploring what it takes to live in a universe where we can each live aligned to our own passions, yet together as one humanity.

We do not make this journey of life alone; we travel together. Every time I felt lost or confused, the next guide or companion appeared eventually. If you are feeling alone, look around you. Who might be the guide or companion that you need? They might be closer than you think. Life would be very dull without companionship to share the laughs, screams, or fears throughout the roller coaster journey of life. We ride it together. The journey toward Wholeness continues indefinitely. I believe we can reimagine life as we want it.

The biggest question is not whether we can have what we want but what is it we *actually* want?

Acknowledgements

If you have read this far, I am extremely grateful to you for taking the time to do so.

I might not have completed this book without the steadfast support from Malcolm Lewis and David Hollands. They both kindly spent many hours with me over several months, continually discussing the book. Malcolm was pivotal in supporting the overall message of the book from the top down, and David got into the details with me that steered the book from the bottom up. With all my heart, thank you. You gave me the confidence I needed to complete this book. Malcolm and David, along with Kate Griffiths, read the entire manuscript, including re-reading revised versions until it was ready.

Thank you to the many who reviewed sections of the book too. My thanks go to:

Ayu Puspita Dewi
Azim Khamiza
Barry Holmes
Becky Kimberley
Doctor Sundara Raman
Dominic Anglim

Ela Staniak
Helen Amery
Janet Hogan
Jos de Blok
Rik Koopmam
Kelly Inwood
Maria Gambin

To all those whom I interviewed, your time is valuable, so I thank you for speaking with me and lending me your stories and insight:

Anita Sathe
Ayu Puspita Dewi
Barry Holmes
Becky Kimberley
Bryant Gallindo
David Beeney
Doctor Sundara Raman
Ela Staniak
Emma Monaghan
Hannah Hardy-Jones
Helen Amery
Jos de Blok
Karen Stover Ministrelli
Kelly Inwood,
Komal Shah
Madelon van Tilberg
Maria Gambin
Marion Child
Osita Aniemeka
Paul Whittering
Pjero Mardesic
Rik Koopman
Rob Ellingham
Roslyn Snyder
Shikha Verma
Sjors de Ruiter
Thom Markham

When I returned to the UK in late 2021, I joined Learning for the 22nd Century (L22c). Within this community, I have had many deep and nurturing conversations that indirectly impacted the writing of this book. My heartfelt thanks go especially to David Hollands, John Savage, John Ssentamu, Matt Piercy, Neena Arakal, Osita Aniemeka, Sufyan Christian, and Thom Markham.

Without all those at New Degree Press, nothing would have been published. I especially want to thank Michelle Pollack for her editorial guidance, and also Eric Koester; it is under his guidance that this book was first initiated into the world.

I am also appreciative of all the early backers of my book. It really meant a lot to me at a time when I was still unsure how the book would actually turn out. Thank you for your support.

Alison Green
Amanda Millward
Andy Gunter
Anna Bakker
Avi Bodha
Barry Holmes
Christopher Brennan
Colin Mair
Cristina Garcia
David Hollands
Dionis Rodriguez
Emma Monaghan
Estelle Pye
Esther Gladman
Evie-May Ellis
Faye Cooper
Felicitas
Frank Bolaji Irawo
Freya MacCormack
Graeme Leese
Irina Shevchuk
Jack Gladman
John Gladman
Julia Robinson
Julia Tegnebo
Julie Sutherland
Kandice Pereira
Kate Griffiths
Katherine Dozier
Katie Jenkins
Katie Wilkinson
Kerryn Vaughan
Koehler
Liesbeth S
Lisa Petrilli
Maria Gambin
Marlies van Wisselingh
Mary Gladman
Mateusz Boszko
Matthew Jarosy
Namit Kathoria
Penelope A Lee-French
Pete Murray
Phil Gladman
Rob Elllingham
Roisin Collins

Sara Asadoorian
Sara Jane Holloway
Gab C. Ciminelli
Sarah Armitage
Sarah Cullen,
Sarah Matthew
Satish Shenoy
Scott Robinson
Sonja Sinz
Usha Mayani
Vasudevan Srinivasan

Finally, I am thankful to myself for continuing until I was ready to publish this book. I am also grateful for the continued support from all those who kept cheering me on at times when I felt overwhelmed.

With immense gratitude,

Luna

Bibliography

Introduction

Limeade. "The Great Resignation Update: Limeade Employee Care Report." 2022. https://www.limeade.com/resources/resource-center/limeade-employee-care-report-the-great-resignation-update/?utm_source=newswire&utm_medium=press_release.

Meadows, Donella, and Jorgan Randers. *Limits to Growth: The 30 Year Update.* Vermont: Chelsea Green Publishing Company, 2004.

Science Daily. "Heart failure cases soar globally." Last modified February 11 2021. https://www.sciencedaily.com/releases/2021/02/210211195326.htm.

Wilkinson, Jonny. "I Am... Rangan Chatterjee" March 24 2022. In *I Am...* Produced by Mags Creative. Podcast, MP3 Audio, https://podcasts.apple.com/gb/podcast/i-am-rangan-chatterjee/id1610549437?i=1000555056633.

World Health Organization. “6 Facts on Obesity.” Last modified June 09 2021. https://www.who.int/news-room/facts-in-pictures/detail/6-facts-on-obesity.

World Health Organization. “Obesity and Overweight.” Last modified June 09 2021. https://www.who.int/news-room/fact-sheets/detail/obesity-and-overweight.

Chapter 5

Crown. “What Is IBS? Irritable Bowel Syndrome.” 24 February 2021. https://www.nhs.uk/conditions/irritable-bowel-syndrome-ibs/#:~:text=There's%20no%20cure%2C%20but%20diet,a%20family%20history%20of%20IBS.

Felitti, Vincent J FACP, Robert Anda, Dale Nordenberg, David Williamson, Alison Spitz, Valerie Edwards, Mary Koss, and James Marks. “Relationship of childhood abuse and household dysfunction to many of the leading causes of death in adults. The Adverse Childhood Experiences (ACE) Study.” *American Journal of Preventive Medicine.* 14, 04 (1998): 245-258. https://www.ajpmonline.org/article/S0749-3797(98)00017-8/fulltext.

Grandi, Dr Giovanni, Dr Ferrari, Dr Anjeza Xholli, Dr Marianna Cannoletta, Dr Palma, Dr Cecilia Romani, Dr Volpe, and Professor Angelo Cagnacci. “Prevalence of menstrual pain in young women: what is dysmenorrhea?.” *Journal of Pain Research,* 05 (2012): 169-174. https://doi.org/10.2147/JPR.S30602.

Jeitler, Michael, Till Wottke, Dania Schumann, Laura M Puerto Valencia, Andreas Michalsen, Nico Steckhan, Martin Mittwede, Elmar Stapelfeldt, Daniela Koppold-Liebscher, Holger Cramer, Manfred Wischnewsky, Vijayendra Murthy, and Christian S Kessler. "Ayurvedic vs. Conventional Nutritional Therapy Including Low-FODMAP Diet for Patients With Irritable Bowel Syndrome—A Randomized Controlled Trial." *Frontiers In Medicine: Gastroenterology*, 08 (2021). https://doi.org/10.3389/fmed.2021.622029.

Chapter 8

Frankl, Victor. *Man's Search For Meaning: The Classic Tribute To Hope From The Holocaust*. Reading: Rider, 2004.

Chapter 9

Cameron, Julia. *The Artist's Way: A Spiritual Guide To Higher Creativity*. London: Souvenir Press, 2020.

Johnson, Dr Amy PhD. *Just A Thought: A No Willpower Approach to Overcome Self-Doubt & Make Peace with Your Mind*. Oakland: New Harbinger Publications, 2021.

Chapter 11

Closer To Truth. "Donald Hoffman - What is Consciousness?" November 22 2020, YouTube Video, 10:33. https://www.youtube.com/watch?v=ynTqCFBhRmw.

Hoffman, Donald. "Do we see reality as it is?" Filmed March 2015 at Vancouver BC. Video, 21:27. https://www.ted.com/talks/donald_hoffman_do_we_see_reality_as_it_is.

Johnson, Dr Amy PhD *Just A Thought: A No Willpower Approach to Overcome Self-Doubt & Make Peace with Your Mind.* Oakland: New Harbinger Publications, 2021.

Chapter 13

Akhtar, Allana. "Elon Musk said a college degree isn't required for a job at Tesla — and Apple, Google, and Netflix don't require employees to have 4-year degrees either." *Business Insider* December 27 2020. https://www.businessinsider.com/top-companies-are-hiring-more-candidates-without-a-4-year-degree-2019-4?r=US&IR=T.

Google. "How we Hire." *Google Careers.* Accessed 13 April 2022. https://careers.google.com/how-we-hire/#step-self-reflection.

Rosefsky Saavedra, Anna, et al. *Efficacy Study Over Two Years.* USC Dornsife Center for Economic and Social Research *Knowledge in Action,* 2021. https://cesr.usc.edu/sites/default/files/Knowledge%20in%20Action%20Efficacy%20Study_18feb2021_final.pdf.

Chapter 15

Department of Defense Dictionary of Military and Associated Terms Online. Edition Ed s.v. "command and control." Accessed June 14, 2022. https://irp.fas.org/doddir/dod/jp1_02.pdf.

Gonzalez-Mulé, Erik, and Bethany S. Cockburn. "This job is (literally) killing me: A moderated-mediated model linking work characteristics to mortality." *Journal of Applied Psychology, 106*,1. (2021) 140–151. https://doi.org/10.1037/apl0000501.

Printed in Great Britain
by Amazon

87842156R00108